"(John) Randall Dennis has given us [...] an aspect of life so few of us fully compr[...] ing deeply from our common biblical [...] with the passion of a fellow seeker and the clarity of a skilled teacher. Employing humor and humility, historical understanding, and Holy Spirit-led insight, he exhorts, encourages, and inspires us to do that for which we all were created—worship!"

—**Marty Goetz, Messianic Jewish singer, songwriter, and recording artist**

"Having known Randall Dennis as a friend for many years it is wonderful to now know him as a writer! The message of this book is profoundly needed. Through the mountains and the valleys, worship is to be our life. May we live it."

—**Rebecca St. James, recording artist**

"I love reading a book that answers the who, what, when, where, why, and how questions related to a particular subject. When that subject is worship, and so many people have so many varying opinions on worship, the answers to those questions often can be (among other things) confrontational and controversial.

Through word pictures of fascinating people and real-life situations from the Bible Randall gives us right (biblical) answers to those questions. He does so with warmth, humor, a deeply communicated passion for and biblical understanding of the subject matter, and (my favorite!) often with tact resembling that of a two-by-four across the forehead!

Thank you, Randall, for reminding us of the power of worship, the responsibility of worship, and the privilege of worship. We all should be more authentic worshipers of Jesus Christ for having read your book."

—**Dennis Worley, music & worship minister, Brentwood Baptist Church, Brentwood, Tennessee**

JOHN | RANDALL | DENNIS

Living Worship

BETHANYHOUSE
MINNEAPOLIS, MINNESOTA

Living Worship: A Biblical Guide to Making Worship Real in Your Life
Copyright © 2004
John Randall Dennis

Cover design by the Lookout Design Group, Inc.

Published by Bethany House Publishers
11400 Hampshire Avenue South
Bloomington, Minnesota 55438

Bethany House Publishers is a division of
Baker Publishing Group, Grand Rapids, Michigan.

Printed in the United States of America

Library of Congress Cataloging-in-Publication Data

Dennis, John Randall.
    Living worship : a biblical guide to making worship real in your life / by John Randall Dennis.
        p. cm.
    Includes bibliographical references.
    ISBN 0-7642-2928-1 (pbk.)
    1. Worship. 2. Worship—Biblical teaching. I. Title.
    BV10.3.D46   2004
    264—dc22   2004012920

Dedication

To my friends at Grace Center/Franklin,

whose deep hunger to worship Jesus

never ceases to amaze and delight me.

JOHN RANDALL DENNIS is a composer, producer, author, speaker, and worship leader. His songs have been widely recorded by nationally known artists, and he has been recognized with various honors: five number-one charting songs, three Gold Record Awards, two Sony-Tree Golden Tree Awards, a song performed for the President of the United States on prime-time television, two Dove Awards, and a Nashville Songwriters Association International Honor. Randall and his family live in Franklin, Tennessee.

Acknowledgments

I would like to acknowledge many who have contributed so graciously to this book:

Kyle Duncan and my other new friends at Bethany House Publishers, who caught my vision early on;

Jeanne Hedrick, a tremendous editor who has been such a blessing as I try to convey my thoughts into a publishable form;

Brian Smallwood and Jeff Dollar, who not only teach me weekly from the pulpit but also humbly model both worship and the spirit of Christ Jesus;

My dear family, who have allowed me many absences to complete this book;

And of course how could I neglect to mention the Holy Spirit? He walks alongside me, helping me each step I take, and challenges me to dare to engage Him, not as a theology or absent member of the Trinity, but as the third Person—an honored Friend.

I am so blessed by all these. And I thank God when I remember them, individually and collectively.

Contents

Transformations

You may have picked this book up in a section of the bookstore labeled "Religion." If so, this book was miscategorized. *Living Worship* won't help you become more religious. Was this book on the shelf marked "Inspirational"? I do hope this book inspires you, but I am not an inspirational writer. "Christian Living"? Well, I suppose it's better than "Christian Dying," but that's not the full picture either. I certainly don't want to merely provide you with more information about God—that might serve only to give you enough ammunition to be dogmatic.

I wish there were a section in bookstores called "Transformation." That would describe my greatest hope in writing this book. My prayer is that the Lord would use what I have written to renew both your mind and your worship. As you begin to see what is meant by worship in the Scriptures I believe you will be excited to enter into that tremendous experience of intimacy with God, your Creator. Psalm 139:14 says that we are "fearfully and wonderfully made." That means we can trust that it is God's desire to shape us into people that both know Him and know how to worship Him in sincerity and in truth.

So how do such transformations take place? One thing is sure: We will need to be willing to repent of our present attitudes and to acknowledge our inability to get it right. Humility will be required to make such an admission, of course. But I have found humility and correction to be my friends since they lead me to the wonderful state called *repentance*. Please don't be tempted to shrink back or be discouraged by this word. Your idea of repentance may not be true repentance at all.

The repentance that God is after doesn't involve shame or remorse. It doesn't involve rending your garments or lying in heaps of ashes wailing. Quite simply, it is a transformation of the mind, a change in how we think about something. When Jesus began his public ministry, His first call to His countrymen was quite simple: "The time is fulfilled, and the kingdom of God is at hand; repent and believe in the gospel" (Mark 1:15). Following this, He began to call His disciples by name. They didn't have to do a bunch of complicated stuff. They simply needed to recognize that He was someone worth following and to change their minds about what the kingdom of God was all about. Repentance and changing our minds to believe in what is true is all that's required for us too. I have come to see repentance, a change of mind, as a very refreshing, joyous thing—not the dreadful picture often painted for us by religion.

The stories of repentance in the Gospels involved celebration and feasting—not fasting and lament. Repentance tastes as sweet as honey. It causes your heart to dance with joy. I like the way it is described in Acts 3:19: "Therefore repent and return, so that your sins may be wiped away, in order that times of refreshing may come from the presence of the Lord." We're going to have to release ourselves from our churchy shackles and wrong ideas if we want to embrace genuine biblical repentance.

Now that I've freely admitted my agenda and my goal, I'll let you in on a little secret: I can't do what I've set out to do. I can't change your mind. I can't transform you. This book is simply that—a book. And I am totally inadequate to transform even the smallest detail of your life. Only God can do that. So (and here's the best part) I have prayed and written this book as an act of faith believing that as you read it, He is going to "show up." I believe He's getting involved with you right now. I've prayed that He will speak to your heart, even when your mind may not fully comprehend something. I believe that the Holy Spirit, as part of a living, communicating, compassionate Trinity, is going to reveal himself in power to you—healing, restoring, forgiving, and transforming you in ways only He can accomplish. As you are transformed, I know that your worship in turn will be transformed. And in that God will receive the glory.

There, I've come clean. You've spent your hard-earned money to purchase a book that can't do anything you need doing, written by someone who can't do any of the things you want done. Doesn't it just make you laugh? So when "the good stuff" happens, you and I will both know that it wasn't this book or this author that made it happen. If you're honest, you'll admit it wasn't because of you either. We'll know it *had* to have been a living, loving God. Isn't that great?

So what's the first step in transforming our worship? The beginning of a transformation in our worship demands that we challenge our preconceived notions about worship. Let me show you why this is important. When someone merely mentions the word *worship*, all kinds of images are conjured up in our minds:

- Hundreds of thousands of churches around the globe conduct weekly "worship services."
- In the East, Tibetan monks worship in majestic mountainside shrines.
- Contemplatives and mystics live in a world of worship, an enigmatic existence.
- The lovesick worship the ground their lovers walk on.
- Americans worship success, power, and affluence.
- Sports fans worship their team and the thrill of the game.
- And the proud worship . . . well, themselves!
- Millions of "praise and worship" recordings are now sold annually.
- Others describe their pursuit of "lifestyle worship."

Are you getting the picture? These confusing and contradictory images point to our problem: We've used and misused the word *worship* in so many ways that the meaning has become obscured. Like *love* and *faith*, the word *worship* has come to mean everything and nothing. What do *you* mean when you say *worship*? There have been countless bloody "worship wars" between Christians who misunderstand the true values in worship and use church sanctuaries as their battlegrounds.

As long as the authentic description of worship is not clearly understood, and as long as there are carnal Christians who think it is about their personal preferences, there will always be subjective arguments about worship. We'll always be distracted by the wrong things if we don't know what we're supposed to be looking for.

Our problem is that the original meaning of *worship* has gotten muddled up with music, praise, prayer, meditation, devotion, and teaching. The church itself has contributed to our confusion by bundling up several corporate spiritual acts in a package and labeling it a "worship service." Millions of us meet weekly for these services that certainly involve worship but are in larger part focused on preaching or teaching. Many Christians use the word *worship* to refer only to the music in church services.

Further, today we are swept up into a worldwide "worship movement" in both contemporary and traditional forms. Praise and worship music ranging from Taizé and chant to over-the-edge rock is in vogue. Youth groups are worshiping quietly in dark rooms with acoustic music and in loud concert-setting mosh pits. Seeker churches sport "worship centers" and are staffed with "worship pastors" and "worship leaders."

If worship plays such a predominant role in our individual and collective spirituality, shouldn't we carefully examine what worship really means? Wouldn't it be great to have Jesus explain what He intended when He said "God is spirit, and those who worship Him must worship in spirit and truth" (John 4:24) rather than what traditions, denominations, and fads have taught us?

Just what is this phenomenon called worship? If this is central to why I was created, I don't want to be muddy in my understanding, do you? We can't afford to use the word *worship* in a cheap or cavalier way.

Abba, we are generations and cultures removed from the worship of the Bible. We need wisdom about worship. We confess with our mouths: We believe your promise that you will freely give us wisdom if we ask. We're asking right now. Please grant us revelation—don't allow us to wander in the blindness of our own faulty understanding or meaningless traditions. Give us a willingness to look at worship with fresh eyes. Please help us to let go of any hardhearted unbelief we're so prone to clutch so that we can embrace truth. We may not have believed before but now we're willing to change.

Your kingdom come—in our worship. Your will be done—in our worship. Just like it is in heaven. Thank you for inviting us to ask. You're the best! You withhold not one good thing from your sons and daughters who ask. What a generous Father we have in heaven! Yours is the kingdom! Amen.

"You will seek Me and find Me when you search for Me with all your heart. I will be found by you," declares the LORD. (Jeremiah 29:13–14a)

CHAPTER 1

Living Words

WE ARE ABOUT TO EXPLORE true stories of worship. I call them *Portraits*. But before these stories can make sense, we need to capture an understanding of the real-life characters we'll be reading about: the ancient Jews of the Bible. We worship the same God they did. They were made out of the same flesh and bones we are, but the miles and generations between us leave us with little common understanding and orientation. Sometimes when I look across a congregation of worshipers today I think we have about as much in common with ancient Jewish worshipers as we do with the Vikings.

Though it's impossible for us to comprehend all the dimensions and nuances of their culture and orientation, can we understand what *they* meant when they said *worship*? Woven throughout the Old Testament stories is a recurring theme of the importance of declarations. In Psalm 51:15 David says, "O Lord, open my lips, that my mouth may declare Your praise." The importance of speaking forth our praise to God is echoed in Psalm 92:1–2: "It is good to give thanks to the Lord . . . to declare Your lovingkindness in the morning and Your faithfulness by night." Isaiah writes, "I will make mention of the lovingkindnesses of the Lord, the praises of the Lord, according to all that the Lord has granted us" (Isaiah 63:7). Why did these worshipers of our God ascribe such importance to speaking out what they knew of Him?

In truth, it would be hard, almost impossible, to overemphasize the significance of words in ancient Jewish thinking and tradition. Their reverence for uttered words is still evident in the lives, families, and synagogues of orthodox Jews today. You and I are twenty-first-century Gentiles—pragmatic "enlightened" Westerners at the dawn of an Information Age. We tend to see words in terms of practical communication. We think words are tools to "get things done" or to express our thoughts and feelings. But the Jews in biblical times saw words in a much different light. They understood uttered words to be living things, almost like entities with a life of their own.

So throughout the Bible we see the enormous significance and impact of spoken words in blessings, in curses, in naming people and places. From the first lines of Genesis through the last of Revelation, words take on this untold importance. The Bible begins with God's words, so potent and powerfully uttered that by fiat alone He could create all that is. Every time "Then God said . . ." occurred, another layer of creation sprang into reality. He simply spoke into existence light and darkness, heavens and earth, plants and creatures. The final book of the Bible, the Revelation of John, proclaims spoken blessings on those who would hear the prophecy of the book and keep what is written (1:3); plagues to anyone adding to it (22:18); and the warning that God would "take away his part from the tree of life and from the holy city" if anyone dared omit some of its words (22:19).

All the stories between Genesis and Revelation underscore the weight of words. Consider a few examples that illustrate this.

Uttered treasures of spoken blessing were considered so valuable by Jacob and his mother, Rebekah, that they were worth stealing. They devised a fraud to steal those treasured words Isaac intended to speak over Esau, Jacob's older brother. Doubly robbed of birthright and blessings (words and their significance), Esau lived much of his life in bitter anguish. (See Genesis 27–28.)

So powerful are words that Balak, King of Moab, commissioned the prophet Balaam to speak curses over Israel to cause their fall in battle. Even God himself considered Balaam's prophetic words so potent that He intervened, keeping Balaam from uttering curses by transforming them into blessings. As Balaam explained to Balak, "I have received a command to bless; when He has blessed, then I cannot revoke it" (Numbers 23:20). So instead of bringing about their defeat—as Balak hoped—Balaam's words actually contributed to Israel's victory!

The weight of words is so great that Paul strongly urged Timothy to avoid worldly and empty chatter because it "will lead to further ungodliness" (2 Timothy 2:16). Jesus warns that those who say "'You good-for-nothing,' shall be guilty before the supreme court; and whoever says 'You fool,' shall be guilty enough to go into the 'fiery hell'" (Matthew 5:22). He also taught that we will be held to account for every idle word we speak (Matthew 12:36). Do we understand the value of our words?

Madeleine L'Engle explores this in her celebrated children's classic *A Wrinkle in Time*.[1] One of her angelic characters emphasizes that you and I literally have the ability to "name" someone—edifying them, building them up, helping affirm them and their future—or we can "X" them—tear down, deny them legitimacy, destroy them.

With this in mind, it's easy to recall many examples in the Old Testament of how the naming of people and places was significant to the Jews. Jabez (literally "affliction") was so named because his mother bore him in extreme pain (1 Chronicles 4:9), and one title attached to the Messiah from Isaiah 7:14, Immanuel ("God with us"), foretold the coming incarnation of Jesus Christ. Can you think of a better name for the original garden that God created than Eden (meaning "delight")? Or consider what God tagged his unique people: Zion ("sunny height").[2] Great care was taken to assign names that captured the significance or essence of the person or place.

To further emphasize this concept, at pivotal points in their lives biblical characters had their original names changed. Genesis 17 is a truly action-packed chapter in which God is forging out the important human lineage through which He would bring forth His Son, the Messiah. In this chapter we see Abram's covenant with God being renewed through the institution of circumcision, a sign that would set the Jews apart from all other cultures. Abram's name is also changed to reflect his new role. Abram becomes *Abraham* (which means "father of a multitude"). His wife, Sarai, has her name changed too, to *Sarah*, which means "princess" in Hebrew. After Jacob's nightlong struggle with the angel of the Lord in Genesis 32, he became *Israel* (literally, "he who prevails with God"). Jesus christened Simon Bar-jona, one of the twelve disciples, *Peter* (meaning "rock" or "pebble"), and after Saul's conversion he was known as *Paul* ("little" in Latin).[3] All of these biblical characters had important parts to play in God's unfolding plan of redemption. It seems both fitting and touching that they would be given new names to reflect God's perception of them and His new plans for them.

What an unfathomable blessing the power of spoken words is to the

Christian! The One whose words matter most in the entire cosmos—the One who uttered worlds into existence—has named us *Beloved*. And if He who bears the highest name calls us *Friend*, it makes no difference if the Deceiver, or a mere mortal, curses us as losers, stupid, unworthy, or anything else. Christ's proclamation of love overrules all such curses because what He speaks over us has the highest authority.

The book of Revelation tells us about a naming to come: Christ promises that if we overcome by faith, He will give each of us a new name. Imagine that! We will be renamed by Him, whose mouth wields a sharp two-edged sword, an image marking the sovereign power of Christ's words. That unique, definitive, eternal name no one else knows—yet it will embody us, becoming our very definition and signify to all who we are.

The truth is we are contemporary Westerners who do not comprehend the value and power of what we're handling: living words. We are like children playing with nuclear warheads and crown jewels. We live in a world of words in abundance. Sometimes I am amazed to consider that I have more words right in my home—published in books and magazines, downloaded, broadcast, e-mailed, text-messaged—than there are grains of sand on a beach. The laptop computer I'm typing into right now has millions of words in it. We say "Talk is cheap." After all, we usually hold things valuable because of their rarity—like diamonds. With so many words, what could they possibly be worth?

In our society we do not comprehend the importance of blessings so we rarely seek them. Our courts are overrun with the litigation of broken contracts (broken words), not the least of which is the oath of love and commitment in our marriage covenants. So it is no surprise that we do not fully comprehend the value of covenant or of Christian rites, though Satanists seem to clearly understand the power of spoken rites and curses.

I should probably make clear here that I am not purporting a teaching that people should expect every foolish or selfish notion they utter to spring into existence. If uttered words worked that way, I'd be flying in my private jet to my private island resort in the tropics right now. There would be no need for me to teach worship. I would simply proclaim that everyone would become biblical worshipers, and it would happen. This is not what I mean by the power of words. We can, however, see the tragic effects of parents who speak over their children words like "You're stupid." Often such children make sure that their parents' words come true. On the other hand, maybe you have seen the healing power of words. Scripture teaches us that by wisdom and blessing "the mouth of the righteous is a fountain of life" (Proverbs 10:11).

You're probably wondering why I'm starting the subject of worship by ranting on about spoken words. It's because uttered words are vital. They are the basic building blocks of worship. I think the particular words these ancient Jewish worshipers uttered will prove to be important clues to unlocking the nature of biblical worship.

No, this isn't a class in Hebrew. And I don't want to try to sound like a biblical scholar—I'm not. I used to think a Greek lexicon was a foreign luxury sedan! Yet it is crucial to look at Hebrew words in order to explore the origins of worship—its original definition and significance. And, for the moment, we need to somehow distinguish Old Testament worship from all the images we associate with worship in contemporary society. So for the purposes of our study I have turned to Strong's Concordance to help me distinguish ancient worship from our contemporary ideas of worship. We'll use the original name: *shachah*.

Shachah

The original Hebrew word we now know as the English word *worship* is *shachah* (pronounced "shaw-khaw"). Theologians tell me shachah is the hitpael form of the Hebrew verb *hishtachavah*. *Hishtachavah* is a term used more than 170 times in the Old Testament. Over and over again this word depicts what the ancients experienced, spoke of, and encouraged themselves and others to do. They "shachah-ed."

But what did shachah look and sound like? How could you tell if someone was shachah-ing? Where did shachah take place? When? How frequently? Did *you* do the shachah-ing or did shachah *happen* to you?

What prompted ancient Jews on their walk home after synagogue on Shabbat to say to one another, "Man, wasn't the shachah just awesome today?" or "I don't know, I just can't shachah when that Asaph teaches us new psalms!" Did some whine that the trumpets were too loud or they shouldn't use timbrel in the shachah service?

Like many other words and names in the Bible, *shachah* describes a physical manifestation that seems to capture the essence of its definition.

It means "to prostrate in honor to God—to bow down, fall down flat, to do reverence, to stoop, to worship"—to shachah. So when you read in the Old Testament that people were worshiping, this was the spirit and posture. It's why you so frequently hear the words *bow down and worship* in the Scriptures as a seamless phrase.

Further, the Bible makes clear what shachah should not be offered to: Shachah should be set apart for God alone. It is idolatry to offer worship to anything created or to false gods. Worship was refused by Peter (Acts 10:25–26), by Paul and Barnabas (Acts 14:11–15), and even firmly refused by an angel (Revelation 22:8–9). We must never offer shachah to other gods, idols, men, or angelic beings. It is forbidden. Both the Old and New Testament Scriptures tell of men who were tried and imprisoned over this very thing—they refused to bow down before a king or emperor (Daniel 3:16–18; 6:11–13; and Acts 5:27–29.)

◆◆◆◆◆◆◆◆◆◆◆◆◆◆◆◆◆◆◆◆◆◆◆◆◆◆◆◆◆◆◆◆◆◆◆◆

WORSHIP IS THE SPIRIT AND EXPRESSION OF BOWING DOWN BEFORE AND PAYING HOMAGE TO GOD.

There is another feature of shachah worth mentioning that I do not believe is eisegesis, "reading into" the Bible text. The posture of shachah not only honors, it is a posture of vulnerability. In brutal ancient Eastern cultures, to bow down before someone paid them homage in such a way as to also express a determined submission. In bowing, the nape of the neck was bared. You placed yourself in a defenseless position. You could not shield yourself nor could you even see what was coming. The one you bowed before could just as easily hack off your head as lay a hand of blessing on you.

All that said, let's start building on this original Old Testament foundation: Worship is the spirit and expression of bowing down before and paying homage to God. For the moment try to forget other images of worship. Strip your mental image of worship's cultural practices long enough to contemplate the spirit of simple prostration. By doing so, we can step back to a time when we're all on common ground—on our knees, on our faces before God.

From this unique vantage point, we'll begin to take a closer look at historical accounts of shachah. We'll trace worship through the old covenant and the new covenant and examine the contemporary expressions we now call worship. In the process we'll sift the original substance from tradition and fad.

Key Points:

Uttered words have untold significance and power.
Worship means the spirit of bowing in homage to God.

Scripture:

Let the words of my mouth
and the meditation of my heart
Be acceptable in Your sight,
O LORD, my rock and my Redeemer.
Psalm 19:14

Questions:

Do I believe that my words are living words?
What do my words (or lack of them) reveal about my beliefs?

✦✦✦✦✦✦✦✦✦✦

ADDITIONAL RESOURCES:

Moore, Beth. *Praying God's Word*. Nashville: Broadman & Holman Publishers, 2000.

Stowell, Joseph M. *The Weight of Your Words*. Chicago: Moody Publishers, 1998.

Telushkin, Rabbi Joseph. *Words That Hurt, Words That Heal*. New York: Quill, 1998.

Portraits of Worship

CHAPTER 2

Worship in Suffering: Job

IN OUR DAY IT IS difficult to imagine a time when the name of Job was not associated with misery. Yet there was a time when the name Job was the emblem of wealth, success, and influence. Job of Uz was a wildly prosperous merchant in a fertile land. He owned vast assets. Thousands of head of sheep, thousands of camels, hundreds of oxen and donkeys, and a host of servants were his. In that day mothers wished their children to be blessed like Job. Fathers dreamt of their sons being so successful. And in that day Job was not only known as a man of immense accomplishment but also widely recognized as a man of integrity. The people of Uz spoke the name of Job in the same breath as the words *honest* and *just*.

The clan of Job was the very picture of abundance! Job had seven sons and three daughters, all healthy, all vibrant, all living mirrors of Job's wealth and success. The family of Job lived full and festive lives, evening after evening throwing lavish parties in each other's homes. (See Job 1:1–5.)

Now, this particular day began much like any other. Job rose early to a clear Syrian sunrise. He offered his usual thanks to God and even offered burnt sacrifices on behalf of his children—just in case one might have sinned inwardly. Afterward he had a bite to eat and went about his business without so much as a suspicion that the coming hours held anything unusual. There were no ominous clouds on the horizon, no sense of foreboding. Even so that same day an unseen cosmic drama was unfolding between the Lord God and the Adversary.

As Job sat down on the porch atop his house he heaved a sigh of deep contentment. All was well. Dusk began to fall and Job rested, drinking in the beauty of the sunset. He smiled at the thought of joining his family later that evening in his eldest son's home for a party. But for now he would simply enjoy a quiet private moment.

Off on the horizon a line of dust caught Job's eye. Gradually Job saw that it was a man in a hot dash, kicking up sand behind him. Curious, Job stood to make out the runner. As he ran nearer Job finally recognized him. He was one of Job's most trusted servants, his face aflame with terror. Bolting up the stairs, in an instant he collapsed before Job, out of breath. "Master, the Sabeans have attacked! They have stolen your oxen and donkeys and have killed the field hands! I am the sole survivor!"

Job sat beside his servant, his mind staggering through the implications of the messenger's words. What an unexpected loss! He considered many options. Should they pursue the Sabeans into their own territory? How quickly could he amass a chase? He stood up and walked to the edge of his porch, scanning the desert with angry eyes.

At that moment Job turned and noticed another runner bolting up the stairs. "Master Job! Master Job!" he shouted. "Good!" Job thought. "Perhaps he's spied the Sabean gang and can tell us where to start the chase." The second runner's news was not good: "Bolts of lightning have struck your sheep and shepherds in the north fields, leaving them torched. They are as ash heaps! I was the only one spared to tell you what has happened!"

Job stared, glassy-eyed, into an empty distance. His assets had dwindled to a third in a matter of moments, and he had no idea what to do. The two messengers remained standing before Job, awaiting his words as a third appeared. "Master! Chaldeans came from three directions, seizing your camels and slaughtering your camel drivers! I alone escaped. What are we to do?"

Job collapsed, dumb struck, holding his forehead in his hand. Never in history had the tide turned so swiftly on a man's wealth in three surging waves! Peering through his fingers, Job realized another servant had silently slipped in behind the others, standing nearby in silence. Tears streaked the dust on the silent servant's face. He was dirty and bleeding. Job continued to peer at him through his fingers, a lump rising from his stomach to his throat.

The servant shook his head, unable to look Job in the eye. He spoke in slow, quiet tones through clenched teeth, "Master! I've come from your son's house. As your children ate and danced, a violent storm swept in and leveled the house. A wall has collapsed on your children and not one of them has survived."

Job struggled to his feet, utterly numb inside. He paced about the roof, his eyes wide and wild, striking terror in his servants' hearts. He stole short fast breaths as though someone had seized him by the throat. Suddenly he tore his robes and disappeared into his house. He needed to be alone.

As the servants wandered one by one down the stairs and away from the house, Job slowly opened the heavy timber door. They froze in their steps and turned to a terrible sight: The ghost of their master slowly and silently emerged from his doorway. His face ashen, his clothes shredded to rags, his head shaven clean—neither beard nor hair, nor even eyebrows, graced his head. Job the impoverished, Job the shattered, Job the ruined collapsed to the ground and worshiped.

"Naked I came from my mother's womb, and naked I shall return there," he said. Despite his fragile mental state Job measured his words with care: "The Lord gave and the Lord has taken away. Blessed be the name of the Lord."[1]

✦✦✦✦✦✦✦✦✦✦

I had never considered Job's story an account of worship until I was researching the instances of shachah in the Bible. I want us to see and touch the flesh of Job. I want us to know he was a real man, not some mythical character. He was a real man in a real crisis. This story is much too large and rich for us to explore it all in detail—the story is worthy of an entire book. But there are some things we can learn about worship from this portion of Job's story.

Right out of the box this first account of shachah shatters any conventional views of "the worship experience." We often picture worship as spilling over the brim of the heart filled with happiness or fulfillment. Maybe we see it as deep, quiet contemplation in a stained-glass-lit experience. Sometimes we romanticize worship as if it were some sacred rapture. This picture severely contradicts all our religious sensibilities. It begs us to ask: What can we possibly learn from Job's shachah?

Worship doesn't have anything to do with our circumstances. In one afternoon he lost it all. He went from "Bill Gates" to an emblem of affliction all in a matter of moments. His worship was just as deliberate and authentic in both states. From our vantage point, it's difficult to remember that Job did not enjoy the benefit of knowing the end of his story . . . just like you and I when *we're* the ones in agony. And Job didn't enjoy scriptural assurances in his dilemma. Job lived before the promises pronounced by prophets; he lived without enjoying the benefits of the Psalms, the teachings of Christ, and the encouragement of the New Testament letters. Yet with what he knew he exhibited an understanding of God and worship that few of us show in crisis.

Let's set aside all the "church-speak" (the expected churchy answers) to challenge my statement: Does biblical worship really have nothing to do with the state of the worshiper? Can we really worship in *all things*, or is this just a religious notion? Can we honestly worship God in sickness, in bankruptcy, or when a relative or friend has died?

Bear in mind, I am not asking, "Can we 'buck up' spiritually?" or "Can we drudge up enough faith to be emotionally confident?" I'm asking, "Can we *shachah* in adversity?" Can we worship authentically when we've received word we have contracted cancer or suffered a terrible financial blow? Can we worship despite the turmoil of a bitter divorce or an unfair accusation? Is it possible to worship in clinical depression or in severe PMS? What if we're in breathtaking chronic pain?

If we are defining worship as the feel-good-all-American-contemporary-or-traditional variety, the honest answer is no. What we call worship in our time and culture, the images we infer when we say "praise and worship" or "worship services," simply do not resonate with Job's shachah. But I want to encourage you: If we are talking about the "real deal," the where-the-rubber-meets-the-road of life, without religious pretense—if we're talking about authentic biblical shachah, that's another matter.

The great news is, if you are in a place where your suffering is unbearable, you can honestly shachah before the Lord. Don't be tempted to think you're being hypocritical, but set your heart to worship despite everything you think, feel, and see. Your worship is legitimate by God's standards, and His is the only measure that counts. Your worship may not fit into the neat little Sunday morning worship boxes you or your church have made, but what's pouring out of your brokenness is real honest-to-goodness shachah.

You may be walking through a chapter of life where you are nearly immobilized by misery. Are your limbs stiffened with terror? Do you wake up in the night with your throat tight, your heart pounding? You may not be able to hold coherent thoughts together, but you can shachah—even if it is only two or three sentences. The record of Job's worship was less than a paragraph, but it was authentic shachah through and through.

WORSHIP DOESN'T HAVE ANYTHING TO DO WITH OUR CIRCUMSTANCES.

We can worship God in the face of financial ruin, in betrayal, through the destruction of divorce, or in intense physical illness. We can bow down before Him, inwardly and outwardly, if we have lost a loved one or if a loved one is lost. In the throes of depression or confusion about God himself, you can still shachah.

Do not be tempted to think Job was superhuman or hyper-spiritual. He was flesh and blood, shredded and poured out. Real, salty tears stung his eyes and streamed down his face. I imagine he heaved deep, confused sighs and had a hard time even swallowing. It seems Job believed it was perfectly consistent to hate what God was allowing, yet worship the God allowing it. Later in the story it seems clear that Job got past this initial shock wave to experience burning anger with God. Yet in this confused anger he did not sin—he still shachah-ed.

When your pain is indescribable and you not only feel broken but you *are* broken, shachah. Bow down and bare your neck to the almighty beautiful Lord whether you're sitting on top of the world or the world's sitting on top of you. You may not be able to control anything whirling around you but you can choose to bow your heart and your posture. Worship is fully within your grasp. Bow down and rest.

Now, if you haven't or aren't worshiping God in the face of torment, I'm afraid I have no condemnation to give you. I've looked all through my religion bag and I'm fresh out of criticism. But when I dug around in there I did find something else—more good news: God isn't the least bit interested in making you feel guilty. He wants you in a no self-flagellation, no moaning and wailing zone, and He wants you to live

WORSHIP IN SUFFERING: JOB

there with Him. He is interested in our recognizing our wrong, verbally expressing it as "confession," and changing our minds and directions ("repentance"). But His first interest is you! That may be difficult to believe in your circumstance but it's true.

Repentance is simple enough, except that you and I are made of arrogant dust. Often our first impulse is to resist admitting when we're wrong. We'd much rather make grandiose religious gestures than to really change our minds. Guilt won't change us for the better. Sheer grit and determination can't transform us. But His love does.

Know well that the Lover of your soul is acquainted with suffering. He knows what it feels like to have the song kicked out of you. This world did all it could to literally beat the song out of Him. And remember that God's children in Babylonian captivity hung up their harps on the willows to weep for a time. They simply could not sing while swallowed up in their homesickness. It's okay.

Please, please do not fear honesty with yourself and your Father in heaven. The world doesn't need spiritual superheroes that deny themselves expression in pain; we've already had our fill of religious superheroes. Christ's church needs *real*, and we need it real bad.

So be honest. Go ahead and do whatever it takes to get in touch with your situation. Tear your clothes. Shave your head. Lie in the dust if you must. I won't tell on you and neither will God. Afterward you'll need to bathe, go shopping for new clothes, and wear a wig for a while—but it's only hair. It does grow back. You can allow yourself to feel the full force of abject brokenness and burning anger—and still worship anyway. You're permitted to be hurt and confused about God and His ways. But when the song is kicked out of you, bleed shachah.

In suffering and weakness you still have the power to proclaim the truth before God and men through worship. You might say, "What God has allowed hurts me beyond description. I don't understand it. At times I feel nothing but pain or anger when I think of Him. Even so, I worship Him in all things."

There is even more good news: Many times when we're numbed by suffering and confused emotions we're convinced we can't hear God. Listen: I believe that urge or impression telling you to bow down is the voice of the Holy Spirit. It may be the first time you've ever really heard Him. I can assure you it certainly isn't the Enemy suggesting you bow down and honor God! This suffering may be the doorway that will enable you to enter more deeply into the kingdom of heaven. Know how I know? I've been there. Done that.

You may think, *But I don't know what to do next when I bow down!* So what? Go ahead and take the first move. You'll never know if there's a second move unless you make the first. Just listen. There may not be a second move. Your worship in suffering is enough. In any case, take heart: God is near and you're hearing Him!

You may have expected something more in worship. You may have expected something different. But this is what you got, at least right now. Please don't let your preconceived notions of God and what it means to be spiritual stand in your way. And rejoice—you are within the sound of His voice. You are in His presence. He is near. Bow down and bless His name. Don't make a religious show of it for others. Don't playact for God or even for yourself. Just bow.

Real worship proclaims real truths. We know that Job fully comprehended the power and significance of his words and actions. There in the dust his first carefully chosen words were a confession of great truth. Despite his circumstance Job recognized the Lord was near in this crisis and he bowed down. He confessed that everything he once owned or had taken away was a result of God's own hand.

Authentic worship confesses in word and song, in physical expression, realities about us and about God. Sometimes the truth spells out the cold hard facts: We will leave this world with no more than what we came into it with. Job also spoke the undeniable truth about God: "God is supreme and He has a mind of His own. He is a wild God that we cannot control. He gives. He takes" (author's paraphrase).

Confession of great truths, in words spoken or sung, is a vital building block of authentic shachah. Unembellished, unvarnished, unrefined, unadulterated truth. Truth doesn't take on self-important, artistic, or intellectual airs. Truth doesn't work itself into a mindless emotional lather. Confession is confession of truth. It pronounces what is. Truth recognizes the glorious attributes of God and confesses those things that we as allies in this new kingdom covenant agree on.

Job blessed the name of the Lord. Job's exact expression uttered Godward was "barak" (baw-rak), or blessing. It fascinates me that his blessing was the very word Satan used in describing God's blessings on Job before the demonic attacks. Satan said God "barak-ed" the work of Job's hands with success and prosperity (Job 1:10). Job blessed God's name, professing God's integrity amid his tragedy.

REAL WORSHIP

PROCLAIMS

REAL TRUTHS.

Such proclamations are consistent with a Hebrew understanding of spoken words. And as confession of truth is uttered, we fire bright arrows of certainty into the face of darkness. Job hurled a proclamation of truth about his predicament and the integrity of God into the darkness of his situation.

Later in the story, Job was tempted by his wife to commit sin. How? By speaking words! "Curse God and die!" she told him (Job 2:9). That's right, he was tempted to speak untruths about God. Still later in the story Job's friends are reprimanded by God himself. Why are they scolded? For the words they uttered! They did not speak the truth about God.

These first two principles about Job's shachah show up again in other biblical stories, such as Paul and Silas: Beaten and imprisoned, they sat in chains and worshiped (Acts 16:23–26). And another profound expression of this type of shachah shows up in the prophet Habakkuk's declaration:

Though the fig tree should not blossom
And there be no fruit on the vines,
Though the yield of the olive should fail
And the fields produce no food,
Though the flock should be cut off from the fold
And there be no cattle in the stalls,
Yet I will exult in the LORD,
I will rejoice in the God of my salvation.
(Habakkuk 3:17–18)

Worship isn't about us or for us. It is about God. Job's shachah was neither about him nor was it intended to be therapeutic—to make him feel better. The next line of Job's story does *not* read, "So Job felt so blessed that he got up and went on with his life with delight, because he worshiped God." Oh, that the human predicament were so easy!

Here is the ultimate irony: We were created to worship God. Worship really does us a world of good, but it is not about us and has everything to do with God—our looking to His majesty, power, glory, and irresistible love. No, worship is not therapy, and it is not spiritual entertainment designed for our preferences, contemporary or traditional.

Unfortunately, the church doesn't help in this confusion. Many well-intentioned sermons and songs are peppered with religious ideas that may feel good but are simply unbiblical and untrue. They say either implicitly or explicitly that all is well with you psychologically and emotionally if

WORSHIP ISN´T ABOUT US OR FOR US. IT IS ABOUT GOD.

all is well between God and you. Some portray worship as spiritual morphine—that if we just praise God the pain will go away.

When Christians get these cues from the church, and the messages don't resonate in real life, it's easy for such believers to become confused and disillusioned. They think God is showing favoritism. After all, since God must be blessing *other* believers and He's not behaving that way toward *them*, God must not care for them. Something must be *wrong* with them. Nothing could be further from the truth! We should weigh each phrase we speak and sing, testing it to see if it is truth, religious sentimentality, or worse yet, a mere religious slogan.

Though it is not our worship of God that aids us, the God of our worship does! Though worship is not for us, the One we worship is. Remember, we are worshiping a real person, and His name is True. There is protection and care in His loving—though not always easy— providence. He has good plans for us, just as Jeremiah said (29:11), and in Paul's words of encouragement, "He who began a good work in you will perfect it until the day of Christ Jesus" (Philippians 1:6). He is worthy of shachah, whether His hands are full of gifts He is about to give us or full of things He has taken from us.

I don't pretend to know why He chooses to give and take. But I have seen His giving and taking glorify Him. It seems that through grace or through miracles, His nature is revealed before our eyes. And whether I understand his motives and ways or not, all of this is still His prerogative. In case you haven't noticed: He's God. Everything is His, so He calls the shots. Of course, the "Where is God in my suffering?" question is legitimate. Job asked it. But it appears Job's questions of suffering are answered outside the scope of shachah.

This much is clear: We shachah, but it is not about us—worship itself is not our focus. It is not the purpose of shachah to entertain us or make us feel good. If shachah does somehow help us emotionally or comfort us in our suffering it is because our very beings are resonating with what we were created for.

Key Points:

Worship doesn't have anything to do with our circumstances.

Real worship proclaims real truths.

Worship isn't about us or for us. It is about God.

Scripture:

Bless the LORD, O my soul,
And forget none of His benefits;
Who pardons all your iniquities,
Who heals all your diseases;
Who redeems your life from the pit,
Who crowns you with lovingkindness and compassion;
Who satisfies your years with good things,
So that your youth is renewed like the eagle.
Psalm 103:2–5

Questions:

Would I have recognized Job's behavior as worship?

Do I honestly see my words and songs in worship as speaking the truth about God?

When was the last time I ever did anything wholeheartedly in worship that was just for *Him*?

◆◆◆◆◆◆◆◆◆◆

ADDITIONAL RESOURCES:

Hillman, Os. *Adversity and Pain: The Gifts Nobody Wants.* Atlanta: Aslan Group, 1997. A good book for businesspeople; it discusses God's purposes through adversity as you walk with Him in the marketplace.

Lewis, C. S. *A Grief Observed.* New York: Harper-San Francisco, 2001. A book that deals with grief over the death of a spouse.

Schaeffer, Edith. *Affliction.* Grand Rapids: Baker Book House, 1993.

Shadowlands. A movie starring Anthony Hopkins and Debra Winger. HBO Studios, 1994.

CHAPTER 3

Worship in Awe: Isaiah

ISAIAH, SON OF AMOZ, was a devout young Judean priest. His days were marked with the disciplines of devotion to God: ceremonial washings, recitations, prayers, sacrifices, observance of all the feasts and holidays. Since he was a priest in Jerusalem he enjoyed these customs in courts of splendor—Solomon's magnificent temple.

The year was 740 B.C. King Uzziah had recently died. It was Rosh Hashanah, the marking of the Jewish New Year. Rosh Hashanah is filled with joyous national-religious festivities. These festivities are traditionally culminated when at an undisclosed time a priest blows the shofar, a trumpet made from a ram's horn, in an unmistakable pattern of mighty blasts. But Rosh Hashanah also initiates the "Ten Days of Awe" leading up to Yom Kippur—days marked with fasting, prayer, and sober reflection on the year past.

On this particular year mixed emotions made the heart of the city churn. Since the Jews had been mourning their king they were eager to part with grief and celebrate, but his death also left them feeling particularly introspective. Isaiah, too, had been reflecting on his life and the state of his heart. While he was not a sanctimonious man, he did try to faithfully observe the Torah. He made continual offerings in the temple. He fasted and prayed.

Dawn was breaking as Isaiah made his way through Jerusalem's stony streets toward the temple. Though the streets were empty he knew the city was teeming with visiting countrymen. Despite its ghost-town appearance the holy city already sounded like a beehive. As he walked, Isaiah heard indiscernible distant voices saying their morning prayers. The air was charged with anticipation. The lots had fallen to Isaiah to have the honor of serving at the table of shewbread. Isaiah's skin literally crawled with excitement.

Approaching Mount Zion, Isaiah feasted on a banquet of sights, sounds, and smells—wisps of incense, piercing flutes and cymbals, sizzling fires of sacrifice, and dancers immersed in echoes of song. This was the magnificence of Solomon's temple. The building itself reflected excellence in its architecture, stone, gold and gems, exotic woods, fine tapestries, and fragrance.

Outside the courts he passed by hundreds of temple singers who broke the chill of the morning by rehearsing an antiphonal psalm. The cantor sang out: "Who may ascend into the hill of the LORD? And who may stand in His holy place?" The choir fired back: "He who has clean hands and a pure heart. . . . He shall receive a blessing from the LORD" (Psalm 24:3–5).

After cleansing Isaiah entered through the massive doors of the temple and walked around a great smoldering altar and up through the porch named Ulam. His destination: the chamber called Hechal, or Holy Place, where Isaiah would prepare the table.

Whiffs of smoky incense followed Isaiah into Hechal. His eyes studied the sights of the hall: the altar of incense, the great table. A large, ornate, seven-branched lampstand of solid gold stood guard before a wall of thick fabric—the great veil separating Hechal from the legendary Godesh Haggodashim, the Holy of Holies. The great veil shrouded the treasured ark of the covenant, where the presence of God was hidden in darkness. The high priest went into that sacred chamber but once a year to atone for the sins of Israel on Yom Kippur. Isaiah was not that high priest, so his focus was on the preparation of the shewbread before him.

Then as quick as a heartbeat it happened. The blast of the shofar. And in that moment the sounds and sights and smells surrounding him became dull and distant. Isaiah's eyes rose from the table to see "through" the dense veil. Isaiah was astonished to be possessed by a vision of the unseen—it was as if he stood on the dark side of the curtain in the holiest room, which was filled with smoke.

And Isaiah saw the Lord. God himself hovered above the ark, and his long, flowing robe filled the entire temple. Two utterly extraordinary angelic beings flew on either side of the Lord. These creatures appeared in shape and texture as natural as any earthly beast, yet the combination of their features was indisputably "otherworldly." Three pairs of wings sprouted from their backs, but only the middle pair held them aloft. With the lowest pair they covered their bare feet in humility. And with the uppermost they sheltered their eyes from gazing directly upon the Lord.

Their beast-man voices declared loud, gleaming truth that broke through the smoke: "Holy, holy, holy is the Lord God Almighty!"—sometimes in unison, at other times overlapping. It seemed they chanted and sang at the same time. Then it seemed like subsonic whispers were emanating from their innermost parts. The deep reverberation of their chant made the solid stone floor shudder to the point that the immense doors of the temple rattled in their posts. Waves of chant swallowed Isaiah up, and he swam in sound as it turned his insides to a quivering mass.

But even all of these were as nothing to Isaiah, whose eyes were transfixed on the Lord himself. At the sight of Him, Isaiah went weak at the knees. Until this moment Isaiah had thought he had learned all there was to know about God from the Law. But now he was encountering the Living One firsthand.

Who could describe Him? There was nothing like the Lord—nothing as beautiful, nothing emanating such waves of authority and love. There was nothing so powerful and pure, mysterious and majestic, nothing even remotely resembling man. Even the shadow of this Indescribable Being far exceeded the greatest glory of an earthly king. Waves of majesty, power, and love emanated from the Lord, sweeping through and past Isaiah.

In an instant Isaiah was undone—not by God's gaze upon him but by his awareness of his sin. The beautiful spectacle of God was more than he could bear, for the Lord was nothing like Isaiah's limited imagination had dreamt Him to be. Sadly, it dawned upon Isaiah that the difference between him and the Lord was unfathomable. This stunned righteous Jew collapsed and began howling, "I am beside myself! I am in anguish because I am a man. I now know I have unclean lips, and I dwell among a people of unclean lips, and I have seen God the King, the Lord of the angel hosts!" He wept and shook in terror and despair.

Then one of the seraphim—the angelic creatures—flew to the altar and with a pair of tongs snatched a live coal. He flew to Isaiah and laid it on his mouth, saying, "Behold, this has touched your lips; and your iniquity is taken away and your sin is forgiven."[1]

✦✦✦✦✦✦✦✦✦✦✦

I see common elements that are foundational between the accounts in Isaiah and Job. Every principle of Job's shachah is consistent with Isaiah's. Let's revisit them briefly:

Worship doesn't have anything to do with our circumstances. Isaiah is in a completely different life situation than Job. There is nothing in Isaiah's story to indicate he was either suffering or sitting on top of the world—he was simply in the "normal" state of humanity. We have no record of Isaiah trying to conjure up this encounter. God chose to reveal himself to Isaiah.

Real worship proclaims real truths. Worship confesses realities about God and about us. While Job's confession was "The Lord gives to me, the Lord takes," Isaiah confessed another aspect of truth. Isaiah's insight was "I am lost. I am a sinner. And I live among sinners. I thought I was okay. But now revelation has changed everything. I can no longer be deluded into thinking I am righteous—I've seen what 'holy' really is" (author's paraphrases).

Worship isn't about us or for us. It is about God. And again we are faced with the irony of our human position: Like Isaiah, we were created for worship. Worship makes us aware of God's goodness. But worship is not about us. It's all about Him. You see, even this story isn't about Isaiah. This story is completely, utterly focused on God. And this God-encounter would become the cornerstone of Isaiah's prophetic ministry.

Isaiah's unique perspective does offer us another layer of understanding about worship.

Worshipers are awed by the "other-ness" of God. They are "awe-able." They are not simply mouthing religious words and routines. They are not looking at their watches to see how long the worship service is running. They are not distracted by the priests. They are captivated by a God who reveals himself. Great worship marvels at a vision of a great God, comprehending and confessing that there is nothing like Him.

There never has been and there never will be. He is entirely "other."

Our imaginings about God fall so short of what He truly is. He is entirely magnificent. He is the God above all gods, kings, rulers, and principalities. He is the all-powerful God of the angel armies, unapproachable light hidden in clouds of darkness. He is, from first to last, entirely "other."

The other-ness between God and us is immense—more than we could ever think to bridge with pathetic religious acts or delusional self-righteousness. Though He is beneficent toward us, and even though He is our dear Father in heaven, let us not be confused: He is utter "other." This is why His willingness to love and care for us is so confounding.

WORSHIPERS ARE AWED BY THE "OTHER-NESS" OF GOD.

And God's "other-ness" is not limited to His omnipotence, His infinite greatness. He is holy. To this day observant Jews recognize this as they acknowledge God's hallowed "other-ness" in the manner in which they refer to Him. To them, even His name is so set apart from all created things that they do not utter it, spelling it as "G-D" lest they somehow profane His name. I am told that because of this the original pronunciation of YAHWEH has been lost. To them, and to Christians, as expressed in the Lord's Prayer, even God's name is hallowed.

Just like you and me, Isaiah had surely heard stories of God and His mighty, wondrous acts of deliverance. He learned much of God—he was a student of the Torah and performed Levitical rites regularly in the temple. But he had never seen God. God was safely hidden away in the next room. A thick veil protected Isaiah from knowing just how different God truly is. One first-person encounter with the Living God shattered all his illusions.

Sometimes people are quick to say they want a vivid God-encounter. They forget that most people who've had a "face-to-face" with Him ended up with broken hips, temporary blindness or the inability to speak, or were asked to walk through extraordinary hardship. As for me, I'm a spiritual chicken. I prefer bowing before a god of my own mental construction and traditions. Please—I'd rather not stand in the presence of the *real* God. Frankly, He's too big and wild for my blood.

In this I am like Susan in C. S. Lewis's *The Lion, the Witch, and the Wardrobe*—I would prefer Aslan was quite safe. Here's how Lewis describes the scene as Susan discovers Aslan actually is a lion:

> "Ooh," said Susan, "I thought he was a man. Is he quite safe? I shall feel rather nervous about meeting a lion."
> "That you will, dearie," said Mrs. Beaver. "And make no mistake, if there's anyone who can appear before Aslan without their knees knocking, they're either braver than most or else just silly."
> "Then, isn't he safe?" said Lucy.
> "Safe?" said Mr. Beaver. "Don't you hear what Mrs. Beaver tells you? Who said anything about safe? Of course he isn't safe. But he's good. He's the king, I tell you!"[2]

God cannot be tamed. And anyone who encounters the God of the Bible will likely hear the clatter of their knees knocking. If they don't, they've either not encountered the real God or they're oblivious.

Worshipers recognize and admit their sin. Here we are faced with yet another perplexing irony: Christians are saints by virtue of our new identity in Christ Jesus. There is no doubt about it—Christ is in us, and we are destined to grow into His likeness. We live and move in humility knowing that we're made of the same mud as all mankind, but we don't focus on our "muddiness." Why? Because God is the object of our worship and He's not focused on our muddiness. He's dealt with it on the Cross. He's moved on to fellowship with us; having redeemed us, He now wants to use us. This is what happened in Isaiah's vision. This is the rest of Isaiah's story.

We are a people destined with a good fate, a destiny that moves us toward the object of our affection. Just as surely as my biological genetics have determined that my son is going to grow up to resemble me, Christ's spiritual genetics dictate that we Christians will continue to grow up to look like our heavenly Father and Elder Brother. Yes, we are saints by our new identity and new future!

Yet we still carry this treasure in vessels of clay. Fallen creatures on a fallen planet sometimes still behave . . . well, fallen. But there isn't any condemnation for our fallen-ness because of Christ Jesus! There may be moments I deny what I am by not grasping I am saved and refined by grace through faith. I may not *feel* saved. But that doesn't change the facts.

When I try to justify and sanctify myself through works I do not bow. I arrogantly stand—justifying myself and elevating myself through self-righteousness. When I defend myself, I have not begun to acknowledge that my best shot at righteousness is filthy rags. And if I cannot recognize those facts of my corruption, I am spiritually deceived.

Isaiah was a man who valued spirituality—a devout observant Jew—he was a priest! And he became a man who could no longer enjoy the indulgent luxury of self-deceit. He had been confronted with the sight and sound

WORSHIPERS RECOGNIZE AND ADMIT THEIR SIN.

of God himself. There was no way he could possibly delude himself with stupid claims of self-righteousness after that.

When God is kept safely in the next room, when there is a thick veil between us, we can pretend the differences between us are maybe not so great. In the outer chamber we can compare ourselves to other mortals, telling ourselves, "I'm not really so bad. I don't steal, I don't commit murder. I honor my father and mother. And I'm much better off than that Dennis fellow—now there's a sinner!"

In the outer chamber it is possible to stand unhumbled. We can be deceived by our lack of revelation and vision. In the outer chamber you or I can think our highly held opinions, goals, and activities are a big deal—until we take a peek through that great veil. Likewise, our worship becomes small when we leave God in the other chamber, focusing on ourselves and our "needs." This is not worship. Let's face it: The cat is out of the bag. When Jesus came to earth everything changed; not only is the veil torn and we have access into the Holy of Holies, but God himself has come out! This is the message of the new covenant, of Pentecost.

It doesn't matter if you're a priest or a prostitute. In Christ's day a "woman of the city" became totally transfixed on the beauty of the Lord, just as Isaiah was. It drove her to shachah—adoring Christ, washing His feet with her tears, and anointing them with ointment. There was no veil between this woman and God. She had a revelation and a vision of Him, while the self-righteous religious types who surrounded Jesus were veiled from seeing His majesty.

They did not join her in bowing down to Him. No, they looked down their noses at this sinner and her worship. Self-righteousness deluded them to the point where they even had the audacity to reprimand God Incarnate for accepting her worship! Go back to Luke 7:36–50, and you'll see it's true!

Christ told us plainly whose prayer is accepted with God. Not the pious, who spiritually elevate themselves and look down their noses at others. God accepts the prayers of people who know who they are and comprehend who He is, then beg for mercy. (See Luke 18:9–14.) *God, grant us all a spirit of revelation so we can see you! We want to join the "woman of the city," Isaiah, and the publican, not the Pharisees and the self-righteous.* When we see who He is and who we are, then we can glory in the glory of Someone Else in us.

We are not justified by our high view of ourselves and our opinions. Not by accomplishments, affluence, or talents. Neither are we justified by our vain efforts to be religious or righteous. Our best shot at righteousness is like rotting rags. No, we are justified when we let go of our religious rags and accept through faith the completed work of Someone Else.

Then faith and grace can suddenly appear. We join the ranks of humbled worshipers like Raphael (the Italian Renaissance painter), who with great deliberation painted himself as one of those raising Jesus on the cross in his *Crucifixion of Christ*, and like actor Mel Gibson, who more recently portrayed the Roman soldier who nailed Christ to the cross in his film *The Passion of the Christ*. We also join the many believers throughout history who admit who God is, who we are and what we deserve, and gratefully accept what He has done for us. Our shachah is genuine and ongoing, not secondhand. It's not just legalistic religious discipline or empty habit.

The best part of Isaiah's story is how he was cleansed and forgiven by the living coals that touched his lips. In the New Testament this is fulfilled in Christ's sacrifice for us. And since our reconciliation is through the beloved Son of the Father, we are not declared acceptable and then merely tolerated. Our Father renames us. We are not His "Enemy"; to Him, we are "Beloved." He "christens" us with names like Special, Dearly Loved, Treasured, Favorite, Precious, Cherished, Son or Daughter. The veil keeping us out has been ripped from top to bottom, and we see the Lord for who He really is. What an extravagant God—what an unreasonable Lover!

Worshipers see themselves as connected to their community. We can recognize the sin of our community and acknowledge our inherent connectedness with it. We Americans are raised to be rugged individualists. Naturally there is a tendency in contemporary American Christianity to see

WORSHIPERS SEE THEMSELVES AS CONNECTED TO THEIR COMMUNITY.

our spirituality as so personal and individual that we lose the awareness of our connection to our culture. True worshipers do not know how to set themselves apart from or above their people. Therefore, they are literally unable to be "holier than thou."

I am forgiven and indwelt. God is leading me from glory to glory, and I am still flawed and fallen. I *can* do all things through Christ, but sometimes I *don't* do all things through Christ. And I have a hunch I am connected to people a lot like me—here in my town, my church, and my family.

I am no better than you or any worse. Neither of us can boast about how we achieved this favored position. We had about as much to do with our spiritual births as we had to do with our physical births. We just "showed up" in the delivery room by cooperating with our mothers and doctors. And we "showed up" in the body of Christ in much the same way—by Spirit-ual delivery. We had so little to do with our spiritual birth. So how can we boast about that? Oh, yes—we can boast in our Deliverer!

And our church is not above the rest of our community. We "catch" our attitudes and sins from our community and culture the same way we catch colds and viruses. We're connected to it in a thousand ways. It's only that we have embraced forgiveness and accepted our adoption into God's family. We are a sinful people. We are a loved people. We are rascals. And we are a forgiven people. We have every reason for hope and optimism. We are people in the process of transformation.

We also have been given amazing new titles, gifts from our God through Christ Jesus: Saints! Sons! Daughters! Wannabe saints strive to be righteous by abstaining from certain acts and foods. Counterfeit saints seek approval from the Father for good behavior and sacrifice. Real saints are forgiven and liberated from the fulfillment of the law and destructive self-righteousness. Real saints not only confess when they commit sins but also confess them one to another! Real saints, abandoning all pretenses of "having it all together," don't need to look spiritual to their communities. Anyone—believer or unbeliever—can get close enough to touch real saints and find out they're made of the same flesh and bone as everyone else.

If we not only claim to believe this but also confess it and live in it, it transforms us and our community. And we can be transformed unashamedly because all of us are in the same state. Suddenly we become a community of saints who are worshiping God in humility, not a community of religious moralizers.

That we have not been justified on our religious performance, that we have peace with God through Christ, that we have access into a standing of grace that we did not conceive, initiate, accomplish, or sustain—these facts should be sufficient cause to make us a community of celebrating worshipers whose fellowship can go on forever!

Key Points:

Worshipers are awed by the "other-ness" of God.
Worshipers recognize and admit their sin.
Worshipers see themselves as connected to their community.

Scripture:

Therefore, having been justified by faith, we have peace with God through our Lord Jesus Christ, through whom also we have obtained our introduction by faith into this grace in which we stand; and we exult in hope of the glory of God.
Romans 5:1–2

Questions:

Am I (and is my church) "awe-able"?
Am I (and is my church) self-righteous?

Do I admit my sin without focusing on it—the way God does?

What sins or attitudes of my community and culture are evident
in my church?

ADDITIONAL RESOURCES:

Miller, Jack. *Repentance and the Twentieth-Century Man*. Fort Washing-
ton, Pa.: Christian Literature Crusade, 2000.

Ortiz, Juan Carlos. *God Is Closer Than You Think*. Vine Books (out of
print; you can acquire used copies through *Amazon.com*).

Ortiz, Juan Carlos. *Living With Jesus Today*. Nashville: Thomas Nelson,
1982.

Piper, John. *A Hunger for God*. Wheaton, Ill.: Crossway Books, 1997.

Wangerin, Walter, Jr. *Ragman and Other Cries of Faith*. New York:
HarperSan Francisco, 2004.

CHAPTER 4

Worship in Abandon: David

BEFORE THE DAYS of Isaiah, a generation before King Solomon built his glorious temple, Israel enjoyed the reign of David. King David governed the people of God in justice and truth, in the fear and admonition of the Lord. And in those days he erected buildings for himself within the City of David. There within the city walls he also prepared a tent, a place of honor, for the ark of the covenant—the box built many years before under Moses' instruction and captured by the Philistines in battle against Israel. After many years without it, David was about to retrieve it for the nation.

Once preparations were complete, King David organized an assembly of Israelites to help bring the treasured ark to its resting place in Jerusalem. Once before David had unsuccessfully attempted to move the ark in a manner apart from Levitical law—moving it by an oxen-drawn cart. The result was catastrophic. When the cart nearly tumbled, Uzzah reached to steady it, and God struck him down for irreverence. The ark then stayed in the house of Obed-Edom, the Gittite, and he and his entire household were blessed for three months. David would not make that mistake again. This time he was careful to move the ark only in the manner prescribed by Moses in the Torah. This time it would be moved on poles carried by men.

To lead the processional, he called together all the descendants of Aaron and the Levites. David appointed more than eight hundred and sixty Levites to consecrate themselves that day because the Lord through Moses had chosen the Levites to carry the ark and minister before Him forever. On the occasion of this grand processional David clothed himself in a robe of exquisite linen as was worn by all the Levites. Underneath this robe he wore a simple linen ephod (apron).

For the occasion the Levites had appointed Kenaniah to lead their choirs in singing, accompanied by lyres, harps, and bronze cymbals. The procession had only taken six steps when they halted to sacrifice a bull and a fattened calf. Once this was done, the procession took its seventh step and the mood of the assembly shifted radically. The air was heavy with shouts and the sound of rams' horns and trumpets, and the processional continued. Caught up in ecstasy, the crowd began to sing louder and faster. Their king led the line, his arms uplifted to heaven, abandoned to laughter and dancing.

Reaching the city gates, the excitement had not worn out the king and his processional—rather, it further energized them. Crowds had gathered for the parade. Men and women, young and old, applauded the arrival of the ark and joined in the joyous dance and song. There David committed to Asaph and his associates a new psalm of thanks to the Lord:

> Oh give thanks to the Lord, call upon His name;
> Make known His deeds among the peoples.
> Sing to Him, sing praises to Him;
> Speak of all His wonders.
> Glory in His holy name;
> Let the heart of those who seek the Lord be glad.
> Seek the Lord and His strength;
> Seek His face continually.
> (1 Chronicles 16:8–11)

David danced, the people shouted. He leapt, they sang. He clapped his hands, they roared with laughter. Finding his royal attire too confining, David tossed aside his fine linen to dance with even more abandon. The streets overflowed with celebration:

> Bring an offering, and come before Him; worship the Lord
> in holy array. (1 Chronicles 16:29b)

From above the streets David's wife, Michal, daughter of Saul, watched the spectacle from a window with steely eyes. Seeing David's reckless joy, she despised him in her heart.

Let the heavens be glad, and let the earth rejoice;
And let them say among the nations, "The Lord reigns."
Let the sea roar, and all it contains;
Let the field exult, and all that is in it.
(1 Chronicles 16:31–32)

The crowd was uncontrollable in their enthusiasm. The ark of the Lord had finally returned! The presence of the Lord himself was in their beloved city. All sang, shouted, and clapped their hands. All were intoxicated with delight. All made a joyous racket—all except Michal, daughter of Saul.

Blessed be the LORD, the God of Israel, from everlasting even to everlasting. (1 Chronicles 16:36)

When the leaders exclaimed "Amen," the people punctuated the finale of David's psalm with "Praise the Lord!" All but the daughter of Saul, that is.

David's heart turned toward his home and his wife. He excused himself, leaving Asaph before the ark. He also left Obed-Edom and his sixty-eight men who had followed in the procession. David left Zadok the priest and his fellow priests to present burnt offerings morning and evening before the tabernacle of the Lord. He left the celebration orchestra and choirs; he left all of the people slowly scattering from the assembly and returned home to bless his family on this special occasion.

Jubilant, David threw open the door to his bedchamber to bless Michal, daughter of Saul. His smile was met by a silhouette in the window—stark, stony, sullen. The dark profile's mockery of her husband was no less sharp than the spears her father had once hurled at David: "How the king of Israel has distinguished himself today—running about disrobed in plain sight of the slave girls as any vulgar fellow might!"

David returned her scorn with the hard facts: "My dance was before the Lord, who chose me rather than your father or anyone from this house when He appointed me ruler over Israel. I will celebrate before the Lord. And I will willingly become even more undignified than this, humiliated in my own eyes. But these slave girls you speak of, by them I will be held in honor."

And Michal, daughter of Saul, had no children to the day of her death.[1]

✦✦✦✦✦✦✦✦✦✦

We read David's psalms and it becomes easier to think of him in the context of personal worship rather than as a leader and king of a nation. I imagine that's because many of his psalms are highly intimate, sharing details of his personal trials and triumphs with candor and passion. But here in 2 Samuel 6 we see David in a corporate worship context. And we are reminded again of the themes we have seen in the other biblical portraits:

Worship doesn't have anything to do with our circumstances. Job's worship was in unmitigated distress and sorrow. Isaiah worshiped trembling. But David's worship, in this instance, represents another dimension of worship—reckless abandon. This story reinforces the fact that worship is not limited to a pious, reflective stoicism. Worship is for every experience in life. Living worship is for all of living.

Real worship proclaims real truths. David's extensive thanksgiving psalm recorded in 1 Chronicles 16:8–36 is well worth examining. Like other psalms it declares many truths about how the weak and wandering nation of Jacob's tribe was given unmerited favor by a good and glorious God. It ascribes many beautiful attributes to our Lord and encourages us to glorify Him, thank Him, and call on His name.

> Let the heavens be glad, and let the earth rejoice; and let them say among the nations, "The Lord reigns" (1 Chronicles 16:31).

So it was that David and the Israelites joyously hurled living words into the air—words proclaiming the goodness of God.

Worship isn't about us or for us. It is about God. It is, in every sense, Godward. None of this celebration clamor was primarily for the Israelites. There was no question this event was a celebration that the Israelites devoted to the Lord. It wasn't about them. It wasn't for them. It was obviously about God.

Worshipers are awed by the "other-ness" of God. As Isaiah would see after him, David and the other worshipers saw God as totally "other." Only God had the ability to deliver and save. Only He kept the Israelites from oppression. They saw God as the One you bring an offering to, bowing down and acknowledging His goodness, His righteous acts, and His holiness.

Worshipers recognize and admit their sin. Worshipers admit they are in community with the unclean. This may be harder to see at face value in this passage because this account is not as blatant as Isaiah's "Woe is me!" But look carefully at David's admonition to the Israelites: "Worship the Lord in the garment of holiness." They did not worship the Lord in striving to be what they were not but in the beauty of His holiness and the holiness in which He arrays His children.

Now we come to the two unique aspects of shachah that can be drawn from David's story:

Worshipers abandon their pride to worship. It is clear David did not care one whit what others thought of him. He was willing to risk looking foolish. Imagine the president of the United States or the CEO of your firm worshiping in abandon despite what citizens or employees or competitors might think of them. We are good at hiding emotions to look the part of the role we play. King David considered it a blessing not to look kingly or like God's chief executive officer. His delight in God eclipsed his concern for decorum.

Does that mean worshipers enjoy carte blanche to do whatever pops into their heads in public worship? Certainly not! Our worship is for God and we mean to draw attention to Him, not distract others by our behavior. But we are willing to ignore what the people above, around, and below us think. Worshipers do not peer out of the corners of their eyes for approval of others. They keep their eyes on the Object of their worship. They have abandoned pride for a greater gift, the full enjoyment of the Lord. They are, as author and pastor John Piper puts it, "Christian hedonists."[2]

We can learn much about this matter not only from this passage but also from the entirety of David's spiritual journal, the Psalms. In his poetic worship journal, there is every dimension of spiritual expression. It is beautiful in its frankness and creativity.

But there is one characteristic that stands out to me about David, which is not solely related to worship.

David understands living worship with living words. He is a spiritual cheerleader for "Team Heaven." He encourages, rouses, and organizes, at times even cajoles people to praise, honor, and worship the Lord:

> Ascribe to the LORD, O sons of the mighty,
> Ascribe to the LORD glory and strength.
> Ascribe to the LORD the glory due to His name;
> Worship the LORD in holy array.
> (Psalm 29:1–2)

> Sing praise to the LORD, you His godly ones,
> And give thanks to His holy name.
> (Psalm 30:4)

The list goes on throughout the Psalms, ending in the glorious Psalm 150—a cheer to praise the Lord in every verse. But there is a further point at which David the cheerleader finds himself in a state similar to Job. Never forget, David wrote some psalms in the caves when he was a refugee and a fugitive. David speaks to his own soul, using self-talk to encourage himself to praise and worship the Lord. These psalms strike me as calls to himself to worship even when he doesn't do it instinctively or feel like it:

> Bless the LORD, O my soul,
> And all that is within me, bless His holy name.
> Bless the LORD, O my soul,
> And forget none of His benefits.
> (Psalm 103:1–2)

That is the technique David repeatedly uses when he is disheartened or realizes he needs to stir up his spirit. He reminds himself of God's blessings and His mighty acts of the past when he doesn't feel like praising Him.

> Who pardons all your iniquities,
> Who heals all your diseases;
> Who redeems your life from the pit,
> Who crowns you with lovingkindness and compassion;
> Who satisfies your years with good things,
> So that your youth is renewed like the eagle.
> (103:3–5)

He utters truth to himself, going on to proclaim the mighty acts God performed for Moses and Israel. Similarly, he reminds himself in Psalm 111:

He has made His wonders to be remembered;
The Lord is gracious and compassionate.
(v. 4)

David goes on to remind himself:

He has given food to those who fear Him;
He will remember His covenant forever.
He has made known to His people the power of His works,
In giving them the heritage of the nations.
The works of His hands are truth and justice;
All His precepts are sure.
They are upheld forever and ever;
They are performed in truth and uprightness.
He has sent redemption to His people;
He has ordained His covenant forever;
Holy and awesome is His name.
(vv. 5–9)

Returning to the unique lessons from David's story of the ark's return in 2 Samuel 6, we must face a sad fact:

Worshipers may receive scorn from the self-righteous. Before looking at Michal, I return you back a few sessions to the woman weeping, pouring herself out at the feet of Jesus. The self-righteous religious types looked down their noses at her and chastised Jesus for allowing her to touch Him. I return you to the Pharisee and the publican. The law-abiding, fasting, praying, tithing Pharisee arrogantly thanked God that he was not like the sinner who sobbed for mercy.

Michal had the utterly foolish notion that David's worship was hers to approve or disapprove of. David recognized that and responded by putting things in perspective: "My dance was before the Lord," inferring it was not for her or any other person to observe but for God. Note that while Michal was David's first wife, in this biblical account she is always referred to as a daughter of Saul, not the wife of David. The implication is that while she is united to David by law, in spirit she despises him— her loyalty still belongs to her father, Saul. This is apparent in David's response to her cutting remarks: "God chose me rather than your father or anyone from his house to bring the ark here" (2 Samuel 6:21, paraphrased).

Sadly, the fact is that even some in the church will scorn people who are abandoned to worship. There are those who are wedded to the body of Christ but hold wrongheaded notions that everyone else's worship must meet their approval. Like Michal, who despised David's reckless, unfettered abandon, they will criticize, maybe even mock, such worshipers. They will expect worship to be done to their standards and preferences. Religious control freaks come unglued at the sight of people who lose themselves in the joy of worshiping God.

Such people are not pleased when they see God affirm worshipers, like He did by choosing David to return the ark. And sadly, just as the Bible noted that Michal, daughter of Saul, conceived no children to the day of her death, those who pass judgment will be spiritually barren unless they have a change of heart.

Key Points:

Worshipers abandon their pride to worship.
Worshipers may receive scorn from the self-righteous.

Scripture:

Sing for joy to God our strength;
Shout joyfully to the God of Jacob.
Raise a song, strike the timbrel,
The sweet sounding lyre with the harp.
Blow the trumpet at the new moon,
At the full moon, on our feast day.
Psalm 81:1–3

Questions:

Do I ever fully abandon myself to the worship of God?
Am I too concerned about what others will think of my worship?

What would be my response if I witnessed my political or spiritual leader worshiping feverishly like King David did?

✦✦✦✦✦✦✦✦✦✦

ADDITIONAL RESOURCE:

Moore, Beth. *A Heart Like His*. Nashville: LifeWay Christian Resources, 1996.

Worship in Warfare: Jehoshaphat

JEHOSHAPHAT WAS THE SON and successor of Asa, King of Judah. By this time the nation of Israel had become a divided kingdom, with the northern regions retaining the name Israel and the southern kingdom becoming known as Judah. Early in King Jehoshaphat's reign he began the process of purging idolatry from his region, in contrast to the more ungodly kings over Israel who saw no conflict between worshiping the gods of other nations and also giving lip service to the God of Abraham, Isaac, and Jacob. In the third year of his reign Jehoshaphat dispatched priests and Levites over the countryside to instruct the people in the Torah. God blessed him and his kingdom with great prosperity, but two subsequent alliances Jehoshaphat attempted with other nations ended in utter disaster.

After the second failed alliance, he joined King Jehoram of Israel in a war against the Moabites, the descendants from Moab, son of Lot, who were under tribute to Israel. This alliance met with success. The Moabites were subdued. But with his own eyes, Jehoshaphat witnessed King Mesha of the Moabites offering his own son as a living sacrifice on the walls of Kir-haresheth—in plain sight of the armies of Israel. The spectacle filled Jehoshaphat with horror and he withdrew to Jerusalem.

Years passed. While Jehoshaphat was preoccupied with instituting reforms, the Moabites seethed in their disgrace. Their defeat was as gravel in their mouths, and they quietly forged a great and powerful confederacy to wage a war of vengeance. The sons of Ammon, together with some of the Meunites, joined the Moabites in an unholy alliance.

Their bloodthirsty eyes were fixed on Judah, on Jerusalem, and on Jehoshaphat.

Some loyalists to Jehoshaphat came with a report, saying, "A great multitude is coming against you from beyond the sea, out of Aram and behold, they are in Hazazon-tamar." The news revived the image of King Mesha's son, a twitching corpse, burning on the walls and in Jehoshaphat's mind. It was as if it were yesterday. "These barbarians," he thought, "are vacant of souls. They are capable of the unthinkable."

Jehoshaphat was full of fear and turned his face to seek the Lord. He proclaimed a fast throughout all of Judah. And so it was that all of Judah united itself in one cry to God. They came together from all the cities to seek the Lord. There in the great assembly, Jehoshaphat stood in the house of the Lord before the new court and cried out to God. This was his prayer:

"O LORD, the God of our fathers, are You not God in the heavens? And are You not ruler over *all* the kingdoms of the nations? Power and might are in Your hand so that no one can stand against You. Did You not, O our God, drive out the inhabitants of this land before Your people Israel and give it to the descendents of Abraham Your friend forever? They have lived in it, and have built You a sanctuary there for Your name, saying, 'Should evil come upon us, the sword, or judgment, or pestilence, or famine, we will stand before this house and before You (for Your name is in this house) and cry to You in our distress, and You will hear and deliver us.'

"Now behold, the sons of Ammon and Moab and Mount Seir, whom You did not let Israel invade when they came out of the land of Egypt (they turned aside from them and did not destroy them), see how they are rewarding us by coming to drive us out from Your possession which You have given us as an inheritance.

"O our God, will You not judge them? For we are powerless before this great multitude who are coming against us; nor do we know what to do, but our eyes are on You."[1]

All of Judah stood there, waiting before the Lord—not merely the men of the assembly, but their wives, their infants, and their children. The air was heavy and still as they waited. Jehoshaphat looked out over a vast sea of faces, a sea of desperation. Tears coursed down faces as they wept in silence.

Then, in the midst of the standing assembly, "the Spirit of the LORD came upon Jahaziel, the son of Zechariah" (2 Chronicles 20:14). This Levite among the sons of Asaph moved his way to the front of the assembly to speak with strength and conviction: "Listen, all Judah and the inhabitants of Jerusalem and King Jehoshaphat: thus says the LORD to you, 'Do not fear or be dismayed because of this great multitude, for the battle is not yours but God's. Tomorrow go down against them. Behold, they will come up by the ascent of Ziz, and you will find them at the end of the valley in front of the wilderness of Jeruel. You need not fight in this battle; station yourselves, stand and see the salvation of the LORD on your behalf, O Judah and Jerusalem.' Do not fear or be dismayed; tomorrow go out to face them, for the LORD is with you."[2]

Jehoshaphat turned and bowed his head with his face to the ground. Then the immediate circle of people around him dropped. Then, like a spreading wave, person after person fell to their faces. And all Judah and the inhabitants of Jerusalem fell down before the Lord, worshiping Him. Weeping and thanksgiving were poured out like oil, for no one doubted that God had answered—and answered with a promise of sure deliverance.

The tide turned as Levites from the sons of the Kohathites and the sons of the Korahites stood up to praise the Lord God of Israel. And the sea of desperation was turned into a sea of praise—a roaring, howling gale of song was heard echoing across the hillsides.

But the story does not end here . . . no, this is just the beginning!

They rose early the next morning and went out into the wilderness of Tekoa. When they arrived King Jehoshaphat stood, and his face shone in the sunlight. "Listen to me, O Judah and inhabitants of Jerusalem, put your trust in the LORD your God and you will be established. Put your trust in His prophets and succeed." He appointed those who sang to the Lord and those who praised him in holy attire, as they went out *before* the army and said, 'Give thanks to the LORD, for His loving-kindness is everlasting.'"[3]

As soon as they began singing and praising the Lord, they set off to do glorious mischief against the sons of Ammon, Moab, and Mount Seir. The LORD set ambushes against them all. Those who came against Judah were routed in a storm of confusion. The sons of Ammon and Moab rose up against the inhabitants of Mount Seir, annihilating them completely. And when they had finished with the inhabitants of Seir, such chaos prevailed that they helped destroy one another!

By the time Judah came to the ascent of Ziz, they looked toward the multitude in shock. They could not believe their eyes. Corpses were lying on the ground, hacked and dismembered. Bodies were impaled against spears jutting from the ground. The soil was drenched in dew and the blood of Ammonites and Moabites. A valley of smoldering silence lay before them, for not one had escaped.

When Jehoshaphat and his people came to take the spoils, they found an incredible bounty of garments and valuables, goods and armaments. The king had to organize the plunder, for it was more than they could carry at one time. The spoils of war were three days in the taking because of the enormity!

✤✤✤✤✤✤✤✤✤✤

This is one of my favorite stories of worship in the Bible. It affects me like few others. It has all the elements of a great story: drama, history, deep spiritual significance, comedy, epic scale battle scenes, the good guys win, and everyone gets rich in the end. What more could you ask for? I know you're probably mystified at how I could find anything comical in this story. I'll get to that later. But right now, maybe the better question is: What can I *learn* from Jehoshaphat's worship?

Worshipers respond to the word of the Lord with deliberate acts of worship. Judah stood at the threshold of total destruction. They had no hope apart from God. Notice that Jehoshaphat did not try to use worshiping the Lord to get out of a jam. He sincerely humbled himself and his people. This act expressed to himself, to his people, and to his God several important points: (1) We are powerless before the approaching multitude; (2) we don't know what to do; and (3) our eyes are on You for deliverance. He sought God's face and inquired of Him . . . and then waited.

It is a humbling thing to be a leader and publicly acknowledge that you have no hope at all unless God acts. There was no Plan B for Jehoshaphat. But God did not keep them waiting. He answered with words of assurance and specific instruction. And with the promise of God came the response of God's people: worship.

With a word from God their circumstance had changed entirely, even though the outcome had not yet occurred. Just the word of the Lord was enough to cause them to fall down and worship Him. What a man of faith Jehoshaphat must have been! Before and after God's promise, the visible facts had not changed. There was not one less man in the opposing army. The insurgents had not retreated one foot. Their intentions for conquering Judah were exactly the same. But the enemy's fate had been sealed without their knowing it.

God, give us such humility in severe trial that we humbly seek you out. God, give us such faith to believe that your promise alone changes everything. God, give us the kind of hearts that respond to your Word with worship. God, give us fearlessness so that we face the morning of trial with deliberate songs of praise. And go before us to defeat all of our enemies while we stand still and see your glory!

WORSHIPERS RESPOND TO THE WORD OF GOD WITH DELIBERATE ACTS OF WORSHIP.

In the face of dire opposition worship requires deliberate acts. They may be planned in advance, or they may be more spontaneous. But I believe the key word is *deliberate*. Jehoshaphat commanded his people to put their trust in the prophet's utterance and deliberately set out to praise God. He put singers before the front lines of his army, thanking God and worshiping Him. By every standard of military strategy, this was madness—unless you really believed the word of the prophet. His promise was "You will not see battle, but see the salvation of the Lord."

What spiritual chutzpah—what faith! Jehoshaphat must have been utterly convinced they would see no battle. Had there been any resistance at all, the singers would have been slain. The assembly of singers in the forces and Jehoshaphat's specific instructions show great deliberation.

In any case, worship demands deliberate acts no matter our circumstance, no matter what emotions may tell us, no matter how ridiculous we look. I call these "simple acts of worship." They could also be called "simple acts of faith." The bowing when our flesh resists. The prayer of thanksgiving for God's promise hurled directly in the face of cancer.

Exultation, though your vine has yielded no fruit and you face possible bankruptcy.

I am not suggesting spiritual dishonesty or hypocrisy. I am suggesting full admission that we have no hope apart from God. I suggest humbling ourselves, seeking His face, and waiting for His word. And when God's promise is given, I suggest performing simple acts of worship that show we *believe* the certainty of God's promise. The acts are not large things—that's why they're "simple acts of worship." But they must be done deliberately. Since we don't applaud "couch potatoes" at home, we shouldn't allow "pew potatoes" at church either.

The body of Christ benefits from the various spiritual gifts of worshipers. If you trace the story, you'll see that from the beginning of Jehoshaphat's reign through to the end, he displayed and used his spiritual gift of administration. The nation obviously benefited greatly from the gift Jehoshaphat used. Just as important, Judah benefited from Jahaziel's gift of prophecy. And Judah was blessed to be led into battle by singers and musicians who were contributing their gifts as well.

There are no gifts we don't need. I greatly need the gifts you contribute to my life and to my corporate worship. You need what I have to offer. We need the gifts of the preacher, the teacher, those with the gift of hospitality, and those with discernment. By embracing one another's gifts, we embrace humility. We say, "We are incomplete without you and what God has given you to share with us."

Glorious Mischief

Finally, I'm sure you haven't forgotten that I said I saw comedy in this story. You probably won't let me get away without letting you in on the joke—but let me assure you that it's a joke that teaches us another important lesson. So let me start by asking you to do this: Close your eyes and dream a moment. What do you imagine God does when we worship Him? He's not proud, so He's not standing nearby gloating and thinking, "Yep, they're right! That's me—Faithful and True, Mr. Almighty Omnipotence! It's about time I got credit for the great job I'm doing." He doesn't feign false modesty either: "Thanks for all your kind words and songs, but I really didn't do that much. I'm just trying to help out a little here and there whenever I can. It was really nothing." So what *did God do* when Jehoshaphat's band began worshiping and praising?

As soon as the people began worshiping Him, He disappeared! Here is a procession of singers pouring their praise out to God, raising banners and making a joyful noise, while He runs ahead. They probably thought He was right there, walking alongside them and drinking in their praise or marching at the head of the line with their procession in His train.

But no—Scripture says that "when they began singing and praising, the Lord set ambushes against the sons of Ammon, Moab and Mount Seir" (2 Chronicles 20:22). I see the Lord running off ahead, laughing at their enemies as He was about to pull off a prank of epic proportions. He not only laughs at our enemies, he laughs them to scorn! (See Psalm 2:4.) No, he's not our grumpy grandfather in heaven, peering over our shoulder, waiting for us to fall short of His glory. That is a false god of our insecure imaginings. He is the Lord of Holy Havoc, the God of Glorious Mischief, our Providential Prankster.

How many times do we think the Lord stands around and drinks in our praise, watching and listening? How many times has He run ahead to run circles around your enemies? Have you ever come to your "ascent of Ziz" and peered over the horizon to see your enemy is no more?

Behold—you are seeing clues that the Mighty Prankster has been at work. The butt of His jokes is your enemy. You need not face every enemy with a knot in your stomach—we don't need to enter the battlefield with faces of flint. We can meet our enemies laughing with heaven.

So what is the lesson here?

We worship a Person. As Christians, we have made much ado about the fact that we are not pantheists—that we do not worship a "force." Eastern religions and New Agers say, "God is a force." We say, "No! God is a Person. We don't worship many gods. We are not pantheists or dualists." We make a big deal out of worshiping one God who has three personalities, and then we often proceed to worship Him as though we worship a mere force or a belief system.

God has a personality! He really is a *Person*. He has preferences. He initiates. He responds—sometimes with an embrace, sometimes with beneficence, sometimes with anger, sometimes with laughter. He communicates. He not only has a personality, He's got "personality plus." In fact, He's got "personality cubed"! He really is worth getting to know.

In the same way, my wife (for me) is worth getting to know. I want to figure out what she enjoys and enjoy it with her. Sometimes I want to do things for her to thank her for something special she's done. Sometimes I want to surprise her "just because." That's because she's an important person in my life, and my simple acts say to her, "I realize you're not just a wife, not just a mother, not a housekeeper or a nurse. You're a person I want to spend time with and get to know."

Are you getting the picture? We worship, as Francis Schaeffer used to put it, "the Infinite Personal God." Both the "infinite" and "personal" are more infinite and personal than we will ever grasp. If we lean toward either in neglect of the other, our understanding is lopsided and our spirituality veers off course. But we do not bow down to stone gods or dead ancestors. We don't bow down to a set of religious rules or worship forms. We bow down to a Person—and a really great Person at that!

Key Points:

Worshipers respond to the word of the Lord with deliberate acts of worship.

The body of Christ benefits from the various spiritual gifts of worshipers.

We worship a Person.

Scripture:

The wicked plots against the righteous
And gnashes at him with his teeth.
The Lord laughs at him,
For He sees his day is coming.
The wicked have drawn the sword and bent their bow. . . .
Their sword will enter their own heart,
And their bows will be broken.
Psalm 37:12–15

Questions:

Are my simple acts of worship executed with great deliberation, or merely as habit?

Do I respond to God's promises with worship?

Do I embrace the spiritual gifts of others?

Has there been a day when I entered a battlefield that God had already won for me?

❖❖❖❖❖❖❖❖❖❖

ADDITIONAL RESOURCES:

Evans, Tony. *The Battle Is the Lord's*. Chicago: Moody Press, 1998.

Frangipane, Francis. *The Stronghold of God*. Lake Mary, Fl.: Charisma House, 1998.

The Hiding Place. A movie starring Julie Harris and Jeanette Clift. Twenty-fifth Anniversary Edition. Bridgestone Multimedia, 1998.

CHAPTER 6

Worship in Perseverance and Humility: Hannah

HANNAH LIVED A LIFE of simple blessedness. But Hannah also led a life of tears. She had no troubling cares for daily needs. Yet the thing she desired most in life she was denied. And that emptiness consumed her—daily. How had such a life of blessing led to such a life of bitter sadness? It began simply enough.

As a young girl, Hannah lived in the green hill country of Ephraim in Ramah. When the young girl became a young lady, she captured the affections of an Ephraimite named Elkanah, the son of Jeroham. A tender, loving courtship led to a betrothal and a joyous wedding. Their life together began with promise, like that of most any young couple. But as the years unfolded it became evident she could bear no children. That fact was certainly not for want of love, for Elkanah loved Hannah as much as life itself. She was his joy and delight. And yet she was an empty vessel.

As the years passed Elkanah watched their youth fading, their house hollow without the laughter of children. He was gravely concerned about his family line being perpetuated. One evening, after prayers were long left unanswered and hope had faded, Elkanah joined Hannah in watching the night sky. The air was thick with the silence of the night. Hannah was quietly staring into the distance as her fingers traced the edge of her robe. Elkanah's face was sullen, his eyes cast to the ground. His words were heavy as they broke the silence: "My Hannah . . . as our customs allow, I have needed to find another wife to bear sons. I have found another wife in Peninnah."

Hannah stopped breathing and stared at her feet. Elkanah continued, "Surely you know that you are the delight of my life. You always will be. Surely you know that my heart will never change." Hannah's chin quivered. Not a word was spoken. There was no seething anger, no emotional explosion. Only the silence after something is shattered, the shards lying on the floor. Elkanah knew full well what his words meant to Hannah. He did not press her by asking her to respond.

Elkanah and Peninnah's betrothal and wedding feast was a public affair. Hannah bore it with grace. But to Hannah's great humiliation, Peninnah became pregnant almost immediately. Not only so, but just as Peninnah's belly grew, so did her pride. She would haughtily parade her budding womb before Hannah when others could not see. As Peninnah's belly and pride increased, Hannah saw Elkanah's joy . . . and her head hung in misery. But this was still not the worst of it. The predicament only became worse for Hannah because Peninnah's womb was prolific! It seemed that no sooner was one child born to Peninnah than she would become pregnant again. And it became obvious to everyone in the house, as well as everyone in Ramah, that the Lord had closed Hannah's womb.

The years passed, each one withering Hannah's hopes and spirit— yet Elkanah's love for Hannah was not diminished. Each year he would lead his house up to Shiloh to worship the Lord of hosts. Each year Eli the priest and his sons would take Elkanah's sacrifices to the Lord on behalf of his family. Each year Elkanah would give portions to Peninnah and all of her sons and daughters. But to Hannah, out of his love and sympathy, he would give a double portion. Each year, seeing this devotion, Hannah's rival would jealously provoke her in spite. Peninnah knew full well that Elkanah's heart was with Hannah, and Peninnah would make her pay for it with bitter, continuous reminders of her barrenness.

So it was that over the years Hannah became weary of seeing the season of worship come. Not for worship's sake, but because these days became to her another poignant reminder of her emptiness. God was to her a provider, a shield, a mighty God—but also the One who had left her fruitless, the One who did not answer her prayer and left her with the consequences. Every year, the script was the same: Hannah and

Elkanah's entire family would go up to the house of the Lord. Peninnah would provoke her. Hannah would weep until she could not eat. Though Hannah honored God in worship and sacrifice, the days of worship represented tears and heartache for her.

Again, this year was no different than the ones before. Elkanah tried to encourage his beloved, saying, "Hannah, why do you weep and why do you not eat and why is your heart so sad? Am I not better to you than ten sons?" After the meal, she rose up and noticed Eli the priest was sitting on the seat by the doorpost of the temple.

Greatly distressed, she prayed to the Lord and wept bitterly. Though no sound escaped, her lips shaped the words in her heart: "O Lord of hosts, if you will indeed look on the affliction of your maidservant and remember me, and will not forget your maidservant, but will give your maidservant a son, then will I give him to the Lord all the days of his life, and a razor shall never come on his head." And as she continued to pray, Eli watched her swaying and moving her lips. It appeared to him that this woman was nothing but a common drunkard on a binge. He was indignant.

"How long will you make yourself a drunk? Put away wine from you!" But Hannah's soft, clear answer turned away Eli's scorn: "No, my lord. I have drunk neither wine nor strong drink, but I am oppressed in spirit. I have poured out my soul before the Lord. Please do not consider your maidservant a worthless woman, for I have spoken until now out of great concern and provocation." Then Eli answered without even knowing the nature of Hannah's prayer. "Go in peace," he said. "And may the God of Israel grant your petition that you have asked of Him." She dismissed herself, saying, "Let your maidservant find favor in your sight."

And then there was an amazing transformation. Hannah went her way and ate her meal without being asked to. Her face was no longer sad. Where there was once nothing but emptiness, now there was a seed of faith growing.

Elkanah's family arose early the next morning and worshiped before the Lord, then returned to their house in Ramah. There, Elkanah made love to his beloved Hannah. The Lord remembered her and made her womb fruitful. Hannah conceived. And in due time, she gave birth to a son and named him Samuel, saying, "Because I have asked him of the Lord."[1]

It would be difficult to read this story and not be moved by Hannah's pain in her unfulfilled dream. Though barrenness has not affected our house, it has touched the lives of several of our friends. It is a heartbreaking situation that many couples face, and the very nature of barrenness strikes at the heart of self-image and relationship. It is a very private condition made very public by its nature.

Since infertility does not strike the majority of us, let me open Hannah's condition to a few more situations that might make us more empathetic and help us learn more from this chapter. If you are physically barren, please know that I do not mean to diminish the scope and nature of your suffering—I am only trying to help more people relate to Hannah and her struggles.

If you identify more with building your career and providing for your family, would it help to draw a picture of barrenness in business? Have you for years thrown yourself with zeal at your occupation, making all the decisions "by the book" yet have seen little or no fruit for your labors? Have you petitioned the Lord for His blessing in a job to no visible avail?

Maybe you have committed yourself to a relationship that despite your sincere efforts to honor that person and to bond there has been little or no fruit. This could be a romantic relationship, a relationship between a parent and child, or one between siblings.

What about your spirituality? Have you sought a genuinely richer, Spirit-led life, and although you have no doubt you are loved by God, your spiritual progress is a constant struggle and does not flourish as you would like it to? Do you sense a barrenness in your spiritual life?

I would like you to relate to Hannah's pain by identifying *any barren place* in your life. A place in which you privately long to see something grow or develop and yet there is emptiness. Every indication of the things around you say "This should conceive; this should grow," and yet it is painfully empty. Perhaps this relationship or situation has been going on for years. It is a constant grind for you, and although you may try to conceal it, anyone who took the time to notice would see you are unfulfilled and struggling. This is the place of your barrenness. And this chapter is for you.

Perseverant Worship Honors God and Gives Us Hope

Perseverance is a quality that God desires all of us to develop. If this were not so, He would not have woven it into the tapestry of the human predicament. If you are a parent (even if you're not, stick with me here), don't you just love it when your children express their love for you? It may be as simple as sitting close to you on a couch or the hugs and kisses they give you before going to sleep. When your child tells you he loves you, doesn't it just melt your heart? Doesn't it transform the moment—spurring you on to express your affections all the more?

But what about the times when for one reason or another you must deny your children something good in itself because you know that it is for the greater good of that child or the family? What about when, even though your child has not gotten the yes from you that he wanted, he continues to honor you with respect and obedience? These are expressions of love and devotion as well.

God delights in your expressions of honoring Him even when your relationship with Him is going through a winter. When you refuse to get tired of doing what is right you eventually receive a harvest of blessing. We are confident of this very thing because we receive such instruction from Paul in Galatians 6:9: "Let us not lose heart in doing good, for in due time we will reap if we do not grow weary." So you see, there's a catch: You can't give up. You have to doggedly continue to utter and demonstrate truth in the face of gray skies and cold winds, even when the cold spell lingers awhile. I believe when your harvest season comes, the blessing is twofold.

First, Romans 5:3–5 shows us how blessings grow when we rejoice in our suffering: "Tribulation brings about perseverance." And then comes the harvest: "and perseverance, [brings about] proven character; and proven character, [produces] hope." Hope is a good thing. It's a blessing that is wrought out of character. Not some mushy, romantic idealism—we're talking about real, rock-solid hope here. And hope doesn't disappoint us. Why? "Because the love of God has been poured out within our hearts through the Holy Spirit who was given to us" (v. 5). Hope is one of those places where the kingdom of heaven is poured out into the kingdom of earth. This is where the unseen meets the seen, where chisel meets stone. And let me point out here that something poured out displaces emptiness, just as light displaces darkness.

If your heart is empty, the love of God can fill it. But we've got to work backward from the blessing. In order for the love of God expressed as hope to fill us we must develop proven character. And to develop proven character, it must be "proven"—we must be perseverant. But to be perseverant, we must have something to conquer. That is the role of tribulation.

Now, doesn't it just stink? Seriously, no! I love the phrase I have heard Joyce Meyer use: "The only way *out* is *through!*" This is the amazing drama of your journey—it's the experience you greatly need. It's the opportunity we have to encounter the Holy Spirit and watch Him work wonders. In that moment when everything around you is screaming, "You're on your own! God won't protect you, He won't provide," you stand amazed, watching God change you, allowing you to see who He really is. The arrows howl as they stream past you; the enemy armies let out a shout as they advance and you stand—worshiping God and becoming stronger for the experience. Greater still, you watch as God's character is revealed before your very eyes. You find out firsthand that He's not who you thought He was at all. He really *is* good. He really *does* provide. He will *not* leave you as an orphan. He *will* come to your aid.

And all of this is only the first blessing.

The second blessing is the actual fulfillment of your desire, the answer to your prayer, the conception of your "Samuel." It doesn't matter how long you've been barren when God moves. And your behavior need not vary from what you've been doing all along throughout your barren years. The change comes when God "remembers" you and circumvents the natural to perform the supernatural. This is the second way the kingdom of heaven is made manifest before our very eyes, right here on earth.

Samuel was not only a blessing to Hannah, he was also a blessing to the entire nation of Israel. What Hannah prayed for and what she got were the same and yet two different things. It's as if she prayed for an apple tree so that she could enjoy its fruit, but God gave her an orchard for everyone to eat from until they were filled.

If you read the rest of Hannah's story (1 Samuel 2:21), you'll see that when she shared what God had given her in Samuel, He gave her three

My mouth speaks boldly against my enemies,
Because I rejoice in Your salvation.

Boast no more so very proudly,
Do not let arrogance come out of your mouth;
For the Lord is a God of knowledge,
And with Him actions are weighed.
(1 Samuel 2:1, 3)

When someone like Hannah walks into the room heads turn because he or she is the very scent of Jesus—who, though He was by very nature God, humbled himself not only to become a mortal but also to submit to a Roman cross.

I encourage you to gaze at Hannah and learn to long for the gift of humility. Search out other great figures of the Bible that really caught God's attention, and if you look carefully you will find them to be humble people. James 4:10 instructs us: "Humble yourselves in the presence of the Lord, and He will exalt you." Read the teachings of Paul, and you will find him emphasizing humility. Look at great Christians of any age who have been used mightily of God and you will find humble people.

Better yet, find those people in your life whom you think smell the most like Jesus, and see if you don't find in them great humility. If you really want to experience God afresh, you will follow those people around, watch their every move, and pray that you learn how they embrace the gift of humility and walk it out. Emulate them. Let their humility rub off on you. Seek every opportunity to hang out with them. I guarantee, you'll *want* to. Why? Because humble people are so *irresistible*.

Imagine you are God for a moment, and you're going to visit a church this Sunday morning. What church would you be most likely to attend? Would you choose it on the basis of its denomination, its size, or whether the people had the most accurate belief system and theology? I hope you know I believe sound theology is important, but I'm trying to make a point. God deals with us as beloved children rather than holding us to Levitical law. Do you honestly think He would choose a church based on their liturgy or lack of it? How about how charismatic the minister is and how inspiring his sermon is likely to be—would that be important to you if you were God? Would God choose a church by taking into account the excellence of the choir or worship leaders?

I believe that the single most important factor to God, the thing most attractive to Him, would be a church that exudes a sense of humility: a place where excellence is embraced but not worn as a badge; a place where theology is soundly rooted in Scripture but no one believes that makes them better than Christians in other denominations. I am not describing false humility that parrots mere words of self-depreciation. I am speaking about people who are unimpressed with themselves, their achievements, programs, and buildings—but totally impressed with God.

The good news is that when God visits your church, He can't sit still in the pew. His love for us makes Him fidget in the pew until He can't stand it anymore—He gets up and begins to touch people. He moves around from person to person, whispering in their ears, touching their hearts, healing their bodies, changing their minds, kissing their foreheads and cheeks, crying with the downtrodden, laughing with the joyful. He is, in the end, from head to toe, a loving Father. And He loves to find humble children with open arms, eager to embrace Him.

Throughout our lives we are sure to encounter seasons of barrenness. The sun will pound down on us as we walk rocky roads. For a time our bodies may not bear children, a relationship will not grow, our business will not yield fruit, our church may languish in problems or fruitlessness. But what will be our response to barrenness? The question is, will we allow our wells of worship to dry up?

I want to encourage you to be perseverant in worship, even though every nerve ending is saying, "God has forgotten me." The facts of the "seen scene" around you simply do not matter—the years of barrenness, the people around you who do not expect your circumstance to change, the brokenness you feel inside. There is an "unseen scene." The mighty God is a loving God. Offer your prayers once again to the One who remembers you. To Him your barrenness is not insurmountable. He is not wringing His hands, pacing the throne room in heaven saying, "What am I going to do? This barrenness is too much for me!"

I do not mean to be insensitive to your barrenness. I have places of barrenness, too, that I implore God to make fruitful. In all I've said my greatest desire is to encourage us both to "put on the full armor of God, so that when the day of evil comes, you may be able to stand your ground, and after you have done everything, to stand" (Ephesians 6:13 NIV). Since this is about perseverance in worship I'll offer my own twist—The King Randall Version (KRV, kinda has a nice sound to it, doesn't it?)—"Put on the full armor of God so that when the day of evil comes you may be able to stand your ground, and after you have done everything, to *bow down and worship*." Then see if just when your circumstances are most painful your Eli does not soon appear, saying, "Go in peace; and may the God of Israel grant your petition that you have asked of Him" (1 Samuel 1:17). And embracing the promise in faith as Hannah did, *your* face will be transformed too.

Key Points:

Perseverant worship honors God and gives us hope.
God finds humble worship irresistible.

Scripture:

For though the LORD is exalted,
Yet He regards the lowly,
But the haughty He knows from afar.
Psalm 138:6

Questions:

Do I really comprehend my perseverance as an opportunity to allow the Holy Spirit to develop character and hope in me?

When I fail to be perseverant, do I live in the assurance that I am embraced and helped by the Holy Spirit rather than judged and abandoned?

Is my church a place where humility is a vital feature?

Do I consider humility valuable in my life and the lives of my family?

◆◆◆◆◆◆◆◆◆◆◆

ADDITIONAL RESOURCES:

Murray, Andrew. *Humility*. Minneapolis, Minn.: Bethany House, 2001.

Peterson, Eugene. *A Long Obedience in the Same Direction.* Downers Grove, Ill.: InterVarsity Press, 2000.

CHAPTER 7

Worship for All Nations: Jesus the Christ

IN 19 B.C. KING HEROD built a temple for the Jews.
This temple was not nearly as grandiose as Solomon's temple of old, but it was much more than Jews should expect from the hands of the Romans. In truth, Herod's gift was no act of spirituality or appreciation. He was a pagan, and there was no fondness between the Roman government and their Jewish subjects. This was only shrewd political maneuvering. Herod kept the Jewish leaders in power. The clerics, in turn, kept the people from rising up against Rome.

Fifty-two years had passed since the temple construction had begun. The Passover was at hand, and a rabbi from Nazareth with twelve disciples pressed toward Jerusalem. What the rabbi found in the temple shocked him—a religious business thriving there in the courts of worship. Merchants sold oxen, sheep, and doves for sacrifices—oxen and sheep to the wealthy, doves to the poor. Money changers sat among tables exchanging various currencies to the temple coin for a tidy profit.

The sight was obscene. The temple, dedicated to prayer, had degenerated into a makeshift market! The rabbi's blood boiled at the sight. He spied a pile of cords in a heap on the stone floor beside one of the merchant's tables. Quietly, he braided together three cords into one.

In a moment, the crack of a braided whip broke the noise of trade. Cord slapped against stone floor and then against flesh. Sheep and oxen, disturbed by the ruckus, rushed about wildly. In their shock and confusion, not one buyer or seller dared to challenge this man.

The man with the whip grabbed bags of money from the tables and emptied them out onto the floor. Pieces of silver and gold rattled on stone, rolling in every direction. In disbelief, the money changers scampered to collect as many pieces as possible without encountering the whip. Then the rabbi grabbed ends of tables and flung them up into the air. Pandemonium reigned.

For just a moment, once the animals had escaped the courts, there was stunned silence as the man with the whip approached those who sold doves. They stood, frozen in place. He looked them straight in the eye and uttered a quiet command: "Take these things away." For a moment they hesitated and looked at each other. Then wisdom prevailed. They gathered their things and made a hasty exit.

The man with the whip raised his voice so all could hear, whether fleeing or remaining to stare at him. With measured words and controlled tone he demanded: "Do—not—make—my Father's house—a—house—of—trade." Nobody doubted his willingness to back his demand with action. He would not even allow them to carry their merchandise through the courts. A few people had gathered at the court gates to peer in at this spectacle, wanting to hear what he would say next. And here was his teaching:

"'Is it not written, "MY HOUSE SHALL BE CALLED A HOUSE OF PRAYER FOR ALL THE NATIONS"? But you have made it a ROBBERS' DEN'" (Mark 11:17).

Crowds were taken aback. Merchants were disgraced. But when the chief priests and scribes heard of this outrage, they were angry. They knew that the man with the whip was shaking the very foundations of their religious system, and they feared he would gain even more followers. In one day this man was transformed from a rabbi to the man with the whip, transformed from merely an irritating heretic to a menace. From this moment on the leaders began seeking ways to destroy him.

✦✦✦✦✦✦✦✦✦

The New Testament was penned in Greek, so the word for worship here isn't *shachah*, it's *proskuneo* (which also means "to bow in homage"). This word conveys an element of affection from a lower being to a higher one. When a Greek person's faithful dog licked his hand affectionately the Greek would say his dog was proskuneo-ing. Got the picture? There are loads of instances where the word proskuneo is used in the Gospels. Here are a few examples:

The Magi: "We have come to Worship Him."

I love these guys! Why? They are the first known Gentiles to get to worship Jesus! Some traditions say they came from Persia, a country familiar with Jewish teaching as a result of Israel's Babylonian captivity. Yet all we know from the biblical account is that through the direction of the Holy Spirit they were able to discern via astronomy that the King had been born. No wonder we call them "wise men"!

Their long journey to Jesus must have been risky and challenging, but the payoff was well worth it. Upon finally finding the holy family, the Scriptures record that "they fell to the ground and worshiped Him. Then, opening their treasures, they presented to Him gifts of gold, frankincense, and myrrh" (Matthew 2:11).

From this account we see clearly that not only is Jesus Christ worthy of men's worship, but also that God has not kept himself solely to the children of Israel. The coming of the Magi to worship is a foreshadowing of Christ's teaching and things to come: Jesus is to be worshiped by all the nations of the world. God himself underscored this fact by taking great steps to make Christ known to Gentiles through wondrous signs.

The Leper: "Lord, if You are willing, You can make me clean."

The biblical narrative (Matthew 8:2) says: "And a leper came to Him and bowed down before Him, and said, 'Lord, if You are willing, You can make me clean.'" Here again, we see the theme reiterated: **Worship has nothing to do with the state of the worshiper.** This leper worshiped Christ in his state of disease and rejection—not because Christ had healed him, not to get a miracle, but because he was convinced this man was worthy of his worship.

The Ruler: "My daughter has just died; but come and lay Your hand on her, and she will live."

I see the **"Real worship proclaims real truths"** theme recurring here in Matthew 9:18 as the ruler utters a deep truth in his worship: "Lay Your hand on her, and she will live." His truth was an expression of faith. And again, the account says the ruler came kneeling and worshiping before Christ *prior* to his daughter's miraculous resurrection— just like Jehoshaphat and the leper had done.

The Disciples: "Truly you are the Son of God."

In Matthew 14 we have the account of Christ walking on water, and Peter, fixing his vision on Him, did likewise. Once the other disciples back in the boat saw this it finally dawned on them that Jesus *really is* who he claimed to be. They proclaimed the truth and hit the deck in worship (v. 33).

There are so many other examples. Both the Canaanite woman whose daughter was demon possessed and the mother of the "Sons of Thunder" (when asking Christ to allow her sons to sit on his right and left in the kingdom) "proskuneo-ed" Jesus. After the resurrection the disciples continued to worship Him in wonder and awe. (See Matthew 28:17; Luke 24:52.)

The stories are beautiful and many, but here's the bottom line: The world enjoyed a day when the object of our worship was physically present. And everywhere He went real people like you and me, those who comprehended who Jesus was, worshiped Him. Wouldn't it have been great to be there? Can you imagine it? I barely can. But it does make me wonder: Would I have been among those people who recognized Him for who He is? And what did their worship look and sound like? Further, would any of us be prepared for what He was about to teach us about worship? Would we be ready for Him to turn worship on its head and make it different from anything we had ever known about it? Well, that's just what He did.

Let's get back to the story: The bottom line in this case really is the bottom line. What Christ taught about worship and the temple is what convinced the religious leaders that they didn't need to control Him— they needed to *kill* him. In fact, Stephen's stoning was based on the same issue. Here's what Jesus said that so unnerved the religious leaders:

1. "Something greater than the temple is here" (Matthew 12:6);
2. "Destroy this temple, and in three days I will raise it up" (John 2:19); and the real kicker,
3. "My house shall be called a house of prayer *for all the nations*" (Mark 11:17, emphasis added).

Worship only needs Jesus. In the same way that we have not understood Jewish worship, it is difficult to recognize the full impact of what Jesus was saying here at first glance. To the religious leaders this teaching could unravel their entire religious/political system. The axe was laid at the trunk of their tree.

Do you recall the glory of Solomon's temple? Well, Herod's temple was not quite as extravagant, but it was nothing to sniff at either. While Jewish worship did occur apart from the temple, the temple was, nevertheless, the focal point of worship—where the presence of God dwelt in their treasure, their temple. It's where the Jews said you *needed* to worship. (Recall the woman at the well in Sychar and her comment in John 4:20: "Our fathers worshiped in this mountain, and you people say that in Jerusalem is the place where men ought to worship.") Herod's temple was the focal point of Jewish national worship—the religious power center where the storehouse was located and the sacrifices, feasts, and religious holidays took place.

What the Capitol building is to the United States government the temple was to Jewish worship. So when Christ's teaching diminished the importance of the temple, it naturally confounded and threatened Jewish leaders. Imagine Congress's reaction to a politician who gains a national following by claiming to be more important than the Capitol, saying that not one stone of the Capitol will be left standing on another! According to Jesus' revolutionary teaching the temple was about to be eclipsed by a Person. The coming kingdom would mean the end of the temple. Jews would no longer make annual trips to Jerusalem and the temple. Christ was teaching that proskuneo (worship) is not dependent on the locality of the temple. Further, He claimed He was greater than the temple! This man said, "Destroy this temple, and in three days I will raise it up" (John 2:19). I think the rulers were deeply threatened by what Christ was saying.

Since these leaders controlled the venue and tools for worship, along with the presence of God in the Holy of Holies, there could be only one conclusion. He was essentially saying, "I'm announcing the new kingdom, which will eclipse your power structure. In my kingdom, you will no longer have an exclusive corner on worship. If I were you, boys, I'd be looking in the help-wanted adverts of the *Jerusalem Post*."

WORSHIP ONLY NEEDS JESUS.

In the coming kingdom, Jesus taught, worship would no longer need the temple or any other physical venue. It would no longer need the familiar instruments of worship such as the burning incense, the table of shewbread, or the golden lampstand. It would no longer demand ceremonial cleansings and sacrifices. Rather, it now demanded a *Person,* and that Person is greater than all of these other things. He is the way. All access to God is through Jesus—anywhere, anytime.

The worship of God is for all nations. Christ not only taught that this House of Prayer was less important than Him; He also said that prayer was not limited to the Jews but was for everyone, changing the customs of Moses. Those disgusting, godless Gentiles (uh . . . that would be me!) would have access to God? And since the temple would not be here, the Gentiles would not have to conform to the Jewish religious system? To the self-righteous elite, these teachings further advanced Jesus of Nazareth to the category of a revolutionary determined to overthrow the entire temple system. He had become a threat, so He must become their target.

Christ was now on their hit list on the basis of these teachings—the same basis for which Stephen was later stoned. What Stephen and Christ both taught was that Jesus fulfilled everything the temple represented, including the place where we stand to meet God. Worship is no longer a ritual at a special time and a special place. Worship does not need a building with inner chambers and priests to officiate a system of sacrifice. The elite were superfluous because worship only needs Jesus. And all nations were welcome and would come to worship Him.

The implications for us are great. There is nothing more sacrosanct about a Sunday morning sanctuary than a Saturday morning on an island in exile. John the Revelator shows us that. Jesus is there. He is because He's *in you*—right? John's great encounter with Christ is not in the temple, not on a high holy day or Shabbat. It was without sacrifice because the Sacrifice had been made. Now you can meet with God anywhere, anytime. We can have access to God in the marketplace, in the hospital, or in the battlefield. And we don't have to be born into a Jewish bloodline. We have been born into a spiritual heritage of freedom through Christ. Royal, priestly, free blood courses through our veins because of His sacrifice.

We have the indescribable opportunity to enter the innermost chamber where God dwells. We have the privilege to get to know Him intimately and find out that He's nothing like what we thought He was when we were imagining Him there on the other side of the thick veil.

There are no longer spiritual power brokers or gatekeepers. You don't need the Pope, Billy Graham, Benny Hinn, your pastor, or *whoever*. There—did I offend everyone? If not, let me press further: You don't need a denomination or rules of conduct, hymns or choruses, organs or drums, hymnals or multimedia in the courts of worship. Are you getting the picture? You don't need formality or informality, the Book of Common Prayer, charismatic utterances, candles, or spotlights. You don't need a cathedral or a worship center or a monastery. All you need is a Person.

Whether your background is Jewish or Gentile, all you need is a Person. You may be a lying drunkard or a hooker who can't shake a cocaine habit. You still just need a Person. You may be a thief, a murderer, or a liar. If so, you're in luck—this Person neglected the righteous elite to hang out with people *just like you*. You may even be worse—you may be a self-righteous religious moralizer. There's hope for you too. The others may get into the courts before you, but if you'll embrace this Person, He won't turn you away. You'll have access to the innermost holy chamber where God dwells. You can worship there.

One of my all-time favorite Bible verses is Galatians 5:1: "It was for freedom that Christ set us free." He did not save you so you wouldn't burn in hell. He did not free you to bring you into bondage to a liturgical order or a spiritual leader. He did not free you to serve. He did not free you for any other reason than that you might taste freedom and feast on it forever.

Go ahead—revel in it! Sing a song of freedom. Dance a freedom dance. Applaud your great Liberator. Laugh as you breathe the fresh air provided by Him! Honor Him by bowing before Him and kissing His hands. Get to know who God really is, rather than relying on second-hand accounts. Yessiree, worshipers only need Jesus. And everyone is welcome, so jump right in! The water's fine.

Key Points:

Worship only needs Jesus.
The worship of God is for all nations.

Scripture:

"I am the way, and the truth, and the life; no one comes to the Father but through Me. If you had known Me, you would have known My Father also; from now on you know Him, and have seen Him."
John 14:6–7

Questions:

Has Jesus Christ liberated my worship from a locality and religious trappings?

How deeply am I in touch with the fact that Christ dwells in me, the temple of my body?

❖❖❖❖❖❖❖❖❖❖

ADDITIONAL RESOURCE:

Jakes, T. D. *Intimacy With God: The Spiritual Worship of the Believer.* Minneapolis, Minn.: Bethany House Publishers, 2003.

CHAPTER 8

Worship in the Spirit: Pentecost

DURING THE EARTHLY MINISTRY of Jesus
Christ his followers heard Him proclaim again and again that a new
kingdom was dawning. It was the kingdom of God here on earth. The
values of this kingdom were different from those of the ecclesiastical
religion taught by the scribes and Pharisees. Jesus taught that to enter
God's kingdom you had to humble yourself and trust like a child. Once
in, you had to hide your spiritual acts and rejoice in being discredited
and persecuted. He welcomed "unreligious" people into this kingdom
with open arms—the unloved, the imprisoned, the tax collectors, the
prostitutes, even the lepers.

In this kingdom He taught that you are blessed when you're at the
end of your rope, when you feel you've lost what is most dear to you,
when you're content with who you are but famished for God. In this
kingdom you forgive people over and over again until well after you've
lost count. You take steps to express love not only to your friends and
relatives but also to your enemies. In this kingdom external submission
to the Law was not the goal; rather, it was releasing the captives of sin,
freeing and healing them so that their inward lives could embrace the
law of love.

His followers could not write off Christ's teachings as romantic idealism or madness. They saw this kingdom unfold before their very eyes:
The blind received their sight, the lame walked, and lepers were
cleansed. The deaf heard, the dead were raised, and the wretched of the
earth learned that God was actually on their side. And the work of the

kingdom was not confined to the hands of Jesus. He instructed His followers to do the same things He was doing, and to their amazement they discovered that *they* could heal people as well. Nobody was as astonished as they were! They watched as Christ tore back the veil of the kingdom of this earth to expose the kingdom of heaven. This heavenly kingdom was being revealed before their very eyes, like another dimension invading this dimension wherever Christ went and wherever they went in His name.

After His crucifixion and resurrection Christ appeared to them in many different settings for about forty days. As they ate meals together and fellowshipped He taught them more about the kingdom of God. One day as they were on the mountain called Olivet, about half a mile outside of Jerusalem, His followers pressed Him about the timing of things. They wanted to know if He was planning to restore the kingdom to Israel right then or at a later time. Jesus answered their questions by instructing them to remain in Jerusalem: "It is not for you to know times or epochs which the Father has fixed by His own authority; but you will receive power when the Holy Spirit has come upon you; and you shall be My witnesses both in Jerusalem, and in all Judea and Samaria, and even to the remotest part of the earth."[1]

And those were the last words He left them with, for just then He was taken up and disappeared into a cloud. This was shocking enough for the disciples, but then two men suddenly appeared wearing white robes. "Men of Galilee," they said, "why do you stand looking into the sky? This Jesus, who has been taken up from you into heaven, will come in just the same way as you have watched Him go into heaven."[2]

So they obeyed Christ's last words to them and left directly for Jerusalem. They returned to the Upper Room they had been using for meetings. There they pledged to one another that whatever happened they were in this together, and they devoted themselves to prayer. They cast lots, asking God to reveal His choice for Judas Iscariot's replacement, and named Mathias among the twelve. The body of believers was about one hundred and twenty in all; this number included some women, Jesus' mother, Mary, and His half brothers.

Forty days passed. Jerusalem was teeming with people from all over who were there for the Feast of Pentecost, or the Feast of Harvest. Pentecost was the third and concluding festival of the grain harvest—a culmination of a season of glad celebration. Parthians, Medes, and Elamites came to join in the offerings, dance, and celebration. Visitors from Mesopotamia, Judea and Cappadocia, Pontus and Asia, Phrygia and Pamphylia, Egypt and parts of Libya, Roman immigrants (both Jews and proselytes), even some Cretans and Arabs—all were visiting Jerusalem to contribute a freewill gift out of the first fruits of their harvest.

The twelve disciples and other followers of Jesus were together in the Upper Room, fellowshiping in one place, when it happened. Nobody was praying or worshiping at the time. But suddenly, without warning, Christ's promise of the Holy Spirit and power came to pass. A deafening roar like a storm swirled through their meeting! No one could tell where it came from. It filled the building and poured out into the streets of Jerusalem. Then, like wildfire, the Holy Spirit came upon the believers and settled over each head with a tongue of fire. As each flame appeared, each person began to speak in a different language as the Spirit prompted him.

When the men visiting Jerusalem heard this riotous wind they came running to see what was going on. A storm? An earthquake? No. As they arrived they were shocked to hear a band of believers praising God—not in their own Aramaic or Greek tongue, but these praises were being fluently spoken in each listener's own mother tongue! The spectators were bewildered. There was no reasonable explanation for this wonder. They kept asking one another, "Aren't these Galileans? Don't they speak Aramaic? How can we hear them describing God's mighty acts in our languages?" Confusion degenerated into argument and accusation. Some taunted, "They've had too much celebration for the Feast of Harvest. They're behaving like drunks on cheap wine!"

It was then that Peter stood up to address them. This man who only weeks before could not even admit knowing Jesus to a young girl now confessed Christ to a multitude of men:

> "Men of Judea, and all you who live in Jerusalem, let this
> be known to you, and give heed to my words. For these men
> are not drunk, as you suppose, for it is only the third hour of
> the day; but this is what was spoken of through the prophet
> Joel:
> > "AND IT SHALL BE IN THE LAST DAYS," God says, "THAT I WILL
> > POUR FORTH OF MY SPIRIT ON ALL MANKIND; AND YOUR SONS
> > AND YOUR DAUGHTERS SHALL PROPHESY, AND YOUR YOUNG MEN

SHALL SEE VISIONS, AND YOUR OLD MEN SHALL DREAM DREAMS;
EVEN ON MY BONDSLAVES, BOTH MEN AND WOMEN, I WILL IN
THOSE DAYS POUR FORTH OF MY SPIRIT AND THEY SHALL PROPH-
ESY" (Acts 2:14–18).

Peter went on to unflinchingly testify how Jesus the Nazarene, a man approved by God with miracles, wonders, and signs, had been crucified by the listeners' consent. He spoke of the resurrection of Christ and His exaltation at the right hand of the Father:

> "Therefore let all the house of Israel know for certain that God has made Him both Lord and Christ—this Jesus whom you crucified" (Acts 2:36).

When they heard his words the multitude was moved with grief—pierced to the heart. Many asked Peter and the other apostles, "What shall we do?" Peter called for a change of their hearts and minds, a change of direction for each of their lives. He instructed them to signify their repentance by being baptized in the name of Jesus Christ for the forgiveness of sins, promising they too would receive the gift of the Holy Spirit.

"Be saved from this perverse generation!" he cried out. And that's exactly what they did. About three thousand embraced his word and were baptized! These entered the new kingdom. Scripture says that the new citizens of the kingdom continually devoted themselves to the teaching of the apostles, fellowship in the breaking of bread, and prayer.

The new church enjoyed fresh blessings every day from the hand of God. Day by day they kept feeling a sense of awe, and many signs and wonders continued to take place through the apostles. They began selling their property and possessions and to share them as other believers had need. Day by day they continued with one mind in the temple, breaking bread from house to house. Day by day they kept taking meals together with gladness and simple sincerity of heart, praising God for having favor with all the people. And day by day the Lord was adding to their number those who were being saved.

✤✤✤✤✤✤✤✤✤

So who is the next great player in this unfolding drama? The Holy

Spirit. And where does He show up? In the temple or on the mountaintop? In a specified form or sacrosanct structure? No. He showed up in power in a room full of believers waiting for Jesus' promise to be fulfilled. Were they performing traditional religious rites or presenting slick religious entertainment? Nope. They were waiting for a Person to arrive, and He didn't let them down.

Just like God the Father and God the Son revealed before Him, the Holy Spirit is a Person, not a force or a mist (though He has manifested himself in such a way that you might think He's a force or a power). The Holy Spirit is a Person who comforts, who heals, One who walks alongside us. Whenever the Father and the Son showed up, things started to happen. And this is true of the Holy Spirit too—when He shows up incredible things start to happen. Why? Because just like real people are active and proactive, the Holy Spirit is a real Person. He does stuff. Wherever He leads, the kingdom of heaven follows, replete with signs and wonders, gifts, and transformation.

Worshipers freely enjoy the Holy Spirit. We know that our loving Father created us and that our "Elder Brother," the Son, freed us through His ultimate personal sacrifice. But what were we created and freed *for*? A Christian waiting room—where we read magazines and keep an eye on our watches until we die? Was all of this done simply to preserve us from hellfire and damnation? No, I don't believe so.

Don't Miss the Good Stuff

We were saved so that we can enter a new kingdom of freedom in the company of a divine Helper and a fellowship of believers. By the invitation of God the Father, and through the sacrifice of God the Son, we enjoy intimacy with our Friend and Comforter, the Holy Spirit, who brings along "the good stuff." Now, if you've struggled with what I have to say about worship thus far, I may really bewilder or frustrate you by my comments to follow.

There was a popular series of Wendy's commercials in the mid-1980s: A grumpy elderly woman named Clara opened the bun on Wendy's competitors' burgers, and searching under the lettuce and pickle, asked, "Where's the beef?"

God provided generously for the Jews for generations, announcing an upcoming special on a free super-size kingdom (enlisting not Dave Thomas, but the prophets John the Baptist and Jesus as spokesmen). God went so far as to make provision for every person to enjoy everything in the restaurant absolutely free—through His Son. God's offering wasn't a Wendy's triple. His offering was a seven-course gourmet dinner. Then He announced a big "Opening Day" event (Pentecost) featuring a special celebrity appearance and free gifts! No wonder He had three thousand people rush in to enjoy his generosity!

Of course I'm offering a ludicrous illustration to drive home a point. We too should be flocking to buy free worship. (Remember the Scripture in Isaiah 55:1? "You who have no money come, buy and eat.") I expect to arrive at my neighborhood establishment and sit down to a big thick, juicy T-bone steak, or at least a triple burger with the beef and trimmings hanging out the edges of the bun. But we are often disappointed. We look at our empty lives and visit so many churches; we open the bun and look under the pickle, and ask, "Where's the worship?" Somehow we're missing out on the abundance that's been provided by God.

We've got more versions of the Bible than we can count, and we've got more Christian entertainment than we need. We've got Christian books beyond number and various translations of the Bible piling up in our homes and offices. We've got fascinating architecture, stained-glass windows, and mesmerizing audio-video systems. We've got candles and incense and comfy seats and carpets. We've got choirs and hymnals and pipe organs and praise teams and choruses with hot rhythm sections. We've got "loud" and lots of it. We can choose from the get-here-early-looking-good-for-the-Lord-and-don't-crack-a-smile service or the come-later-as-you-are-and-bring-your-feelings-on-your-sleeve service. We run services by the book or freewheel and work 'em up into a lather. But I keep looking under the pickle for the Person.

The "beef" is missing. And it's missing in our churches because the beef is missing in many of our individual lives. We think people won't notice what's missing if we pile on more lettuce and tomato. We distract ourselves from the vital issues of worship we've discussed and make noise about service logistics so we won't hear our hearts crying for a Person.

If we don't recognize the vital need for authentic worship, if we're worshiping in a form (whatever your form is—and you *do* have one) without a Person, then it's no wonder many people are left to nitpick over the style of music, the excellence of the performance, or the length of the teaching time. No wonder there are arguments over whether the bun should be whole wheat or white with sesame seeds, whether there should be more mustard or less ketchup. The main ingredient is missing and nobody wants to say, "Wait a minute—where's the *beef*?"

Imagine something with me for a moment. Let's say you have a good friend—someone you look forward to seeing at Starbucks for a cup of coffee and to chat awhile. Let's imagine you enjoy him because he is extremely creative,

◆◆

WORSHIPERS FREELY ENJOY THE HOLY SPIRIT.

insightful, and empathetic to your challenges in life and also has a great sense of humor. What if every time you hung out with him he had a really great insight about you and your life? What if he continually showed you that all your stark, legalistic preconceptions about God were "outer court" misconceptions and that He's not at all like you thought He was? What if frequently when you got together to visit, your friend brought you gifts that he had specifically chosen just for you and your family? What if that friend was of significant political and business influence and was willing to command his emissaries to cast influence to help you at your place of work or when you travel abroad? Wouldn't you be *eager* to welcome such a friend? Come, Holy Spirit!

Now, would you set up a weekly get-together with such a friend (at Starbucks, of course) without the expectation that he would show up and speak to you? Would you plan your get-together in such a way that inferred or showed plainly that you expected him to do nothing but sit silently at another table? Would you go on with your get-together ignoring him, saying, "I really don't expect or want you to express your creativity, insight, or empathy, and frankly I don't believe you have a sense of humor—I've got a book about God, so I'd rather interpret it than ask you, the God in my book"? Why would you *not* want those gifts he chose specifically for you and your family?

This is the dilemma of many Christians and consequently the dilemma of many churches. Either we don't desire or we don't believe that the Holy Spirit will show up if we throw Him a party or invite Him over to our house for coffee. We don't believe He'll do the things He said He'd do if we lay hands on the sick and preach the good news of a new kingdom of freedom. I could spin this in a thousand different ways and dance around the subject, but here's the unvarnished truth: If we are not freely enjoying the Holy Spirit in private and corporate worship there can be only two possible reasons: our arrogance or our unbelief. I've encountered them time and again as I have visited churches across the nation. I've encountered them time and again in my own heart.

There is an arrogance of life that infers by our choices that we don't need the Holy Spirit to be active in our daily lives and churches. And in the case of unbelief, I've found two types at work: (1) unbelief that the Spirit wants to or will actually show up; or (2) unbelief expressed as fear of what the Holy Spirit will do or might lead us to do. The latter is an unbelief that the Holy Spirit's character is what the Bible says it is. We feel that if we lose control of our lives and worship services we might find that the Holy Spirit will take us to places that are strange and unpleasant. In either case, we wittingly or unwittingly build up walls of form and preference to resist Him. We're unbelievable, unbelieving control freaks.

So what are the signs indicating that the Holy Spirit is present in our lives and in our worship services? What helps us see and feel that we're enjoying the freedom that we were intended for? Is it the goose bumps we get when we hear that magnificent pipe organ? Is it the excitement we feel when that mind-blowing media system knocks our socks off? Is it related to whether or not we adhere to a traditional liturgical form or the one we made up? (Every church I've ever encountered has a liturgy; some are written down, some aren't.)

Is our worship supposed to show signs of tradition, reflection, meditation, and intelligence *or* relevancy, energy, excitement, and emotion? These are essential questions behind the issues fueling "worship wars" in some circles. Musical style is just a manifestation driven by larger questions. Many times it becomes the ignition point because it so emotionally embodies these questions and issues.

I submit to you that we're looking at the wrong things. All this noise is again distracting us from the absence of a Person. I have found the Holy Spirit alive, present, and at work in traditional churches; I have also found Him in seeker churches and in postmodern worship services. I have found Him absent in all of these, too—no matter how reflective and insightful, no matter how pumped-up and emotional, no matter how biblically accurate the services may be.

These were the signs of the Holy Spirit's presence and power in the early church (Acts 2:42–47):

- devotion to the teaching of the apostles;
- ongoing fellowship in the breaking of bread;
- sincere prayer;
- a continual feeling of awe concerning the person of God and what He was doing in their lives;
- signs and wonders;
- generosity to those in need;
- unity;
- gladness and simple sincerity of heart, praising God for showing favor with all.

What happens in a church like this? Day by day the Lord adds to their number with more who are being saved. These are not formulas, but the vital signs of life in our spirituality and in our churches. When any of these are missing, our lives and churches are not only lopsided and wobbling, we're missing out on something vital. I'm not trying to establish a "New Testament Eight Commandments." I'm just trying to provide practical ways to recognize the activity of the Holy Spirit in your life or the life of your church.

When Christianity was Hellenized during the reign of Constantine the house church was diminished by the growth of the large, well-funded institutional church. Christianity was no longer a sect of Judaism but a governmentally ordained religion in its own right. Though we have been blessed in that metamorphosis, somehow through the ages we've lost the organic vitality that marked the early church. An understanding of the value of the spiritual gifts of hospitality, generosity, and simple sincerity has diminished. Every time you see the eight vital signs in an individual life or church you see spiritual and tangible growth. Every time they're missing you'll see increasing apathy, pettiness, atrophy, illness, and eventual death.

Experiencing the Really Real

Let me digress a minute. Ever since I was in college I've had a sense that this world is real and spiritual things are "really real." That is to say we live and work in a world that appears real, and it is. (If you don't believe it's real, just ask the dentist to do a root canal without Novocain and this world's reality will become painfully real right away.) But the kingdom of heaven is like another dimension that is even more real than the real things around us. And sometimes the things we see and experience in this real world are manifestations of the eternal world that is even more "real." We don't always recognize or properly interpret eternal things in this real world when we experience them.

I'd compare the difference between real and really real to the difference between two-dimensional and three-dimensional objects (I can hear you now: "I can't believe he's using geometry to teach worship. I *knew* I should have bought *The Purpose-Driven Life* instead!"). This illustration explains the unexplainable spiritual things we encounter. It's like we're living in a two-dimensional world experiencing three-dimensional objects. What do two-dimensional beings think they're seeing when they encounter a (three-dimensional) sphere passing through their flat, two-dimensional world? They think they're seeing a circle changing sizes right before their eyes—a miracle! It's not really a miracle—it's quite natural to the three-dimensional world. But it's extraordinary to two-dimensional beings.

I experience the "really real" when God miraculously heals someone right before my eyes or provides a job for the jobless. I experience the really real when someone renounces the kingdom of darkness as they step into the kingdom of light. I experience the really real when I am honored to hold someone's hand and pray for them as they lie in a hospital bed writhing in pain. I experience the really real when the Holy Spirit helps me see a truth in a biblical text that I have worn out through familiarity or misuse.

I am grieved by what I see in churches, and in my own heart and that of my family, when I only encounter real things. I feel short-changed. I expect to see real things, but I also expect to see really real things—pieces of the next dimension. I believe the descriptions of the early church I listed are really real things. If you know anything about human nature you'll have to admit that they don't happen naturally in our churches and in our lives. And when anyone, believer or unbeliever, sees the really real, it is irresistible. You can't box the really real into meetings on Sunday mornings. The really real occurs in the workplace, in our schools, in the grocery store, in Starbucks. You saw the really real in each of the Portraits of Worship—in Job, Isaiah, David, Jehoshaphat, Hannah, and Jesus, and in the coming of the Holy Spirit.

These really real things make absolutely no sense in the economy of this world. They are, in a post-Christian society, countercultural. But they are essential to the economy of the kingdom of God. I imagine they are a picture of the really real, the next dimension, right here in our real, current dimension—a heaven on earth. But the really real is what we're called to be co-laborers in. We remain here now to follow the Lord's lead in establishing His kingdom here, until "the kingdom of the world has become the kingdom of our Lord and of His Christ" (Revelation 11:15).

Yes, I'm grieved when I do not recognize or encounter the really real in my worship and in the worship of a church I'm visiting. But grief does not captivate my imagination. I am captivated by the really real and a conviction that the kingdom of heaven is increasing, not decreasing, right here on earth. There are places on earth that delight in seeing His will done as it is in heaven. I see an ongoing expansion of God's dominion as the Lord of the angel armies tears down unseen principalities and demolishes every thought that raises itself above the knowledge of Christ.

Let me leave you with a final element in the story of the second chapter of Acts. Ever wondered about those tongues of fire above the believers? What is their significance? What gives?

The vital clue can be found in the dedication of Solomon's temple. If you look at the account of the dedication in 2 Chronicles 7:1–2, the Lord's grand arrival was marked with fire from heaven. It was His demonstration that He accepted this temple and that His presence was entering the Holy of Holies. It was witnessed by everyone in attendance. I am not an Old Testament scholar, but I was once told by one that subsequent to the dedication of Solomon's temple new temples were dedicated by building *a small fire of dedication on the roof*. This was how they commemorated that spectacular, really real event.

It doesn't take much imagination to understand the significance of what happened at Pentecost. I believe the Holy Spirit was saying, "My temple is in these believers. I have arrived." This is consistent with the rest of New Testament teaching about worship, Christian living, and the new temple being made up of individual believers (see Ephesians 2:21–22). This does not negate the importance of a physical house of prayer in its proper context. But the Holy Spirit does say, "I don't live there. I live in people—that's where I make my home." Don't you know that your bodies are the dwelling place of the Holy Spirit? (1 Corinthians 3:16; 6:19, paraphrased)

God the Father had been dwelling among men in a temple set apart—veiled from us and us from Him. God the Son sacrificed himself to give us access to that holiest of holy chambers, so His Father ripped the curtain separating us—all the way. We can approach the mercy seat without obstruction, but we must remember that the inverse is also true. God's dwelling place among men is not limited to that chamber anymore. God the Holy Spirit comes rushing over those who believe on the name of Jesus, and God dedicates us—His new temple—with fire (Matthew 3:11).

We were built for His pleasure, to worship Him and enjoy Him. We were cleansed by the blood of Christ and dedicated to God. And now the Holy Spirit has come to dwell in His temple.

Key Point:

Worshipers freely enjoy the Holy Spirit.

Scripture:

Do you not know that you are a temple of God and that the
Spirit of God dwells in you?
1 Corinthians 3:16

Questions:

Do I recognize the *person* of the Holy Spirit?

When was the last "really real" moment in my life?

How am I in touch with the fact that Christ Jesus is my high priest and the Holy Spirit resides in my "temple"?

◆◆◆◆◆◆◆◆◆◆

ADDITIONAL RESOURCES:

Cymbala, Jim. *Fresh Wind, Fresh Fire*. Grand Rapids, Mich.: Zondervan, 1999.

Evans, Tony. *The Fire That Ignites*. Sisters, Ore.: Multnomah Publishers, 2003.

CHAPTER 9

Worship of Heaven: John

IN THE FIRST CENTURY the Romans began to
enforce the cult of emperor worship. Christians faced ever-increasing
hostility because they refused to bow down to Caesar. Among the
devout was a man named John. Because of his staunch defense of God's
Word and testimony of Jesus and the new kingdom, he was exiled to a
penal island called Patmos. Whether John was a man frequently given
to visions we do not know. We do have a spectacular vision he carefully
documented in the book of Revelation. It is clear and detailed. I am
compelled to believe we must either embrace it in its entirety or dismiss
it as the ravings of a lunatic.

"I was in the Spirit on the Lord's Day, and I heard behind me a loud
voice like the sound of a trumpet, saying, 'Write in a book what you
see, and send it to the seven churches.'"[1]

John claims to have had a visitation by the glorified Christ, who
shared words of encouragement and warning to the seven churches of
Asia. And then John had a vision of a door standing open in heaven,
an opportunity to see the future and to see the very throne room of the
eternal God. John's account pulls back the gray veil of the uncertain to
vividly reveal the really real. Please ask the Lord to help you picture this
vision in your mind with me, for we have an opportunity here to peer
into eternity. This is his account (in my words):

A throne stands in heaven, and He who sits on it is like a jasper
stone and a sardius (a ruby, garnet, or some other red gem) in appearance. A rainbow surrounds the throne, like an emerald in appearance.

If you recall, the rainbow is a reminder to God himself of His promise to never again destroy the earth by flood. His promise ever surrounds Him. Flashes of lightning emanate with peals of thunder from His throne, and seven lamps of burning fire are before it—the seven Spirits of God. Surrounding the throne are twenty-four thrones, each with an elder seated on it. These elders are arrayed with the finery of white garments and golden crowns.

Before the throne is a crystal sea and in the center, around the throne, are four heavenly beings. The first creature resembles a lion, the second a calf, the third has a face like that of a man, and the fourth is like a flying eagle. Each of the four creatures has six wings and is full of eyes, around and within.

Day and night they unceasingly utter these words:

> "HOLY, HOLY, HOLY IS THE LORD GOD, THE ALMIGHTY, WHO WAS AND WHO IS AND WHO IS TO COME" (Revelation 4:8).

And as these creatures give glory, honor, and thanks to Him who is seated on the throne, all twenty-four elders rise from their thrones and fall down before Him. They worship Him, casting down their crowns before the throne, saying,

> "You are worthy, our Lord and God, to receive glory and honor and power, for you created all things, and by your will they were created and have their being" (Revelation 4:11 NIV).

These creatures and elders are unselfconscious. They are, with every atom of their being, utterly transfixed on the unbelievable One in whom we have put our trust. They see Him face-to-face. This is their worship.

✦✦✦✦✦✦✦✦✦✦

The book of Revelation is a book of encouragement, instruction, and warning to churches. It is also clearly apocalyptic—John was granted prophetic foreknowledge of real things that had not yet come to pass. But even more so, it is a book of worship.

Heaven is a real place—more real than the community where you're reading this book right now. Have you seen it or touched it? No. Can we see or feel the radio waves flooding our bodies at any given moment? No, but both are there, I assure you. Turn your radio on or dial a number on your cell phone and those radio waves will become tangible. There are a number of people—both in the Scriptures and otherwise—who claim to have visited the place called heaven. I guess they had their radio tuned to the right frequency!

Is there focused, intense worship in heaven? Yes. Can I see it? I have not as yet. Nor have I seen firsthand the regal pageantry of the weddings of England's royal family. But just because I haven't witnessed one of them does not mean they did not happen. In the same way, I must never define the reality of God's kingdom by the limitations of my own experience.

Those who inhabit heaven enjoy the worship of God without peering through a glass darkly. They don't need to look at mountains and oceans and skies to see His fingerprints—clues to His existence—because they are present with Him. They realize in fullness. They do not need to push aside the distractions of the ordinary, like business appointments, pressing errands, and rumbling stomachs begging for lunch. They know the sheer joy of tasting and touching and smelling and hearing and seeing without the demands of faith. And someday you will too, when you are an inhabitant of heaven.

But for now we are told that we are blessed if we *don't* know these things firsthand and yet believe. Though we must wrestle against the demands of the real, we also know His grace is present and sufficient for this moment. And through the gift of faith we can engage in the worship of heaven here on earth. By grace, through faith, we can embrace the really real as the God of heaven inhabits us.

We have been instructed to pray a proclamation: "Your will be done, on earth as it is in heaven" (Matthew 6:10). I believe it is plain that God's will is that we worship Him in spirit and in truth. When we agree with this prayer we acknowledge our submission to His lordship in this place and agree with God's intentions for us here. Then we will begin to see God granting us the worship of heaven on earth. But we must start with this prayer (which Christ posed as a proclamation of faith). I believe that unless we do so, we are powerless even to recognize the kingdom of heaven and the worship of heaven, let alone *embrace* it. We are hopeless unless the Lord grants us revelation. So what is the worship of heaven like?

The true God on the throne is at the center of worship. He is at the center among the heavenly beings; he is at the center of the twenty-four elders. Later when John sees a multitude beyond number from every nation, made up of all tribes and peoples and tongues, it is the One on the throne at the center that is the focus. It is to Him that they wave branches and cry out with a loud voice: "Salvation to our God who sits on the throne, and to the Lamb" (Revelation 7:10). This is the satisfaction of Christ's proclamation that the kingdom is for *all* the nations.

All the angels are standing around the throne with the elders and the four living creatures. John sees them fall on their faces and worship the One in the center of it all—the one on the throne: "Amen, blessing and glory and wisdom and thanksgiving and honor and power and might, be to our God forever and ever. Amen" (v. 12). What a picture. What a sound. And you thought *The Lord of the Rings* was an epic!

As we worship here on earth as it is in heaven may we always guard the throne. Let us never allow anything or anyone to ascend the throne of our hearts or to capture our attention. Let us shun idolatry at all costs—most of all when it comes dressed in religious robes. We worship Him who is at the center—not a form, not a belief system. We don't worship angels; we don't worship the Bible; we don't worship denominations, and we don't worship saintly people. We do not worship composers or their works, Christian celebrities, or religious leaders or their teachings. We certainly must not worship worship! We worship Him who is on the throne at the center of everything.

We "ascribe to the Lord" all the attributes that are due Him: the thanksgiving, honor, power, blessing, glory, and salvation. All of it! We take no pride in our human religious efforts or past accomplishments—they are rags that we swapped for His righteousness. Our works, even we ourselves, are eclipsed by our obsession with the One on the throne. We are lost in His presence entirely because we know who He is and what He has done.

We must be sure that the God in the center of our worship is the true and living God—not a god of our religious misinformation or carnal mental constructs. We must not worship a god that we *think* we know, but the God who really is. We need to freely acknowledge that the God who is and the god of our minds or traditions may not (in fact, *do* not) entirely match up. He's not the latest "fad god," shaped by our current culture's expectations and norms. No, He's no "designer god." We can't sell Him on an infomercial because He won't fit in a box.

I say again, "He is a Person" and a BIG person, at that. He is active—not a passive entity, a force, or a belief system. And since we recognize our understanding of Him is finite and flawed, we must humble ourselves and be open to the possibility that at any moment He might reveal a new dimension of His nature to us. We know this "new" God that reveals himself may not match up to the little god we've worshiped all these years. Surely you experience this every time you read the Scriptures and some passage you've read since childhood leaps off the page—suddenly the revelation about Him contradicts the God you believed in before. Usually we try to skirt such passages by putting on our blinders of tradition. We would rather deal with "God the story" than to actually encounter and deal with a living person this powerful. But sometimes we're open and vulnerable. Sometimes we actually allow Him to renew our minds and ponder, asking the Spirit, "What are you trying to show me here? Who are you—really? You're not who I thought you were at all!"

Is your God wringing his hands because of the pickle you're in? Then your God is too small, too weak to command angel armies. Is your God waiting for you to sin so He can dole out His judgments and wrath? Then your God is too petty and too quick to anger. Is the God you worship holding grudges? Is He uninvolved with your life? If you worship the God revealed through Jesus Christ the answer will be no to all of the above. Jesus was approached by the needy and He continually asked, "What can I do for you?" One final question: Do you imagine that your God is rushing off to run the universe, lacking the ability to be intimate with you and accept you? If so, you made that God up or accepted a false image of God passed on to you by someone else.

I am not saying to open yourself to every kooky wind of doctrine—be rooted in the God of the Bible! But I *am* saying that the God you may have been taught may not be an accurate reflection of the God of the Bible. George MacDonald used to preach that it is worse to hear of Christ wrongly than to never hear of Him at all. If the Christ you have heard of is anything less than God and Love Incarnate, I urge you: Start over. Sit down with your Bible and ask God to help you learn as if you've never heard of Jesus. Keep a notebook, and as you begin to meet the real Christ jot down His personal characteristics (including the things He's *not*). Write down the Scripture reference so you can go back to it later. You'll be astonished to discover who He really is.

Even people who have walked faithfully with God for years need fresh truth to renew their minds. We all need to be transformed through a renewed relationship with Him. We need to be pruned of our misbeliefs and unbelief, to be watered by the Word, and spoken to by the Spirit in order for fresh spirituality to grow. Such was the case with Jeremiah. Though he was devout in his walk with the Lord for many years, there was a time when he struggled greatly with the Lord. When he prayed, God essentially said, "If you change your mind about Me, then I will restore you—if you extract the precious from the worthless, you will become My spokesman" (Jeremiah 15:19). These are the moments when God is telling us, "Sure, I love you and we have been friends—but you've got to be open to the fact that who I am and who you *think* I am are two different things. Your thoughts about me are in error and you'll need to change them before you can be effective in my kingdom."

When you know who He is in truth, it will be nearly impossible to resist worshiping Him in truth. He's just that good. You will not be able go through the motions or merely mouth words like "blessing and honor and glory and power." You will deeply desire to ascribe these things to Him. The God who is really real has a personality that will surprise you. He is more loving than you thought, more embracing. He's not trying to get you to do a lot of churchy stuff. In fact, you may find Him not to be very churchy himself.

Sometimes He's simply trying to get you to hold still long enough for Him to embrace you. And He may embrace you longer and closer than you're comfortable with. He's not really interested in all the self-righteous pretense that you were absolutely convinced would earn you spiritual brownie points. You'll find Him enjoyable to spend time with; you'll even discover He's got a sense of humor, which will really toast all of your rigid presuppositions.

Key Point:

The true God on the throne is at the center of worship.

Scripture:

And a voice came from the throne, saying, "Give praise to our God, all you His bond-servants, you who fear Him, the small and the great."
Revelation 19:5

Questions:

If someone I know told me of such a vision as John's, what would be my reaction?

Is the true God the center of my worship?

When was the last time I allowed the Spirit to open my eyes to a new revelation about Him?

❖❖❖❖❖❖❖❖❖❖

ADDITIONAL RESOURCES:

Lewis, C. S. *The Great Divorce*. New York: HarperSan Francisco, 2001.
Peterson, Eugene. *Reversed Thunder*. New York: HarperSan Francisco, 1991.

✦✦

Living Worship

✦✦

CHAPTER 10

Living Worship

IF YOU'RE OBSERVANT, you will have noted that I jumped right from Pentecost to Revelation without breathing a word about worship in between—the right-here-where-we-live section. You weren't going to let me get away with that, were you? "Okay, why the leap?" you ask. Because that's exactly what the Bible does!

Have you ever noticed that the apostles' letters make virtually no mention of "worship services"? The book of Acts tells us that the first believers still went to worship in the temple. (Yes, while Christ taught that He was greater than the temple, he didn't teach that worship there should be abolished.) We've also noted that believers also met in homes to pray and enjoy one another's fellowship.

Though my first inclination is to wish the New Testament provided us clear pictures of personal and corporate worship, I've come to be glad it does not. This is consistent with the pattern of the new covenant of love, the new kingdom of freedom. As a people in the new covenant we no longer rely on a system of rules or Levitical rites. We rely on a relationship. The Word is inscribed on our hearts and we walk "in the Spirit," in love. Levitical worship was a picture of eternal, personal worship. But we don't legalistically adhere to a prescribed worship system; we worship individually and corporately as we live and move in and with a Person. We worship in spirit—we worship the true God in humble freedom. We embrace both order and freedom.

After His ascension Jesus was no longer physically on earth with us. The physical object of our worship was missing. He had already announced a coming change in worship orientation to the woman at the well: "An hour is coming when neither in this mountain nor in Jerusalem will you worship the Father" (John 4:21). This is a central theme in Christ's teaching on worship. And then Jesus unshackles worship in one key proclamation: "An hour is coming, and now is, [revealed in me] when the true worshipers will worship the Father in spirit and truth; for such people the Father seeks to be His worshipers" (John 4:23).

Remember that originally believers had no gatherings called "worship services" in the New Testament. They worshiped in the temple and shared Communion and fellowship in one another's homes. This explains the deafening silence and lack of instruction regarding Christian corporate worship. Apart from a few directives Paul wrote about propriety in gatherings (such as in 1 Corinthians 11 and 14) there is nothing—and you could probably make the case that those gatherings were not worship services per se. In the book of Revelation worship reappears as people bow down to God in heaven. But everywhere in between, we are confronted with a glaring absence of *proskuneo* and *latreuo* (another Greek word for worship). Are you up for a good detective story? This is what I call "The Case of the Missing Worship." Let's look at the clues:

In Paul's letters *worship* appears but once—when an unbeliever falls down under the power of prophecy (1 Corinthians 14:25). In the letters of Peter, James, and John worship is never even mentioned. Can you believe it? Doesn't this missing worship cause you to wonder? If not, take your pulse for signs of life—this is a vital clue.

When Paul speaks of worship he doesn't refer to a specific location or form for worship. He refers to a spiritual experience—treating all of life as an act of worship when lived in the awareness of the really real. Here are some more clues that point to "living worship":

> I urge you, brethren, by the mercies of God, to present your bodies a living and holy sacrifice, acceptable to God, which is your spiritual service of worship. (Romans 12:1)
>
> For we are the true circumcision, who worship in the Spirit of God and glory in Christ Jesus and put no confidence in the flesh. (Philippians 3:3)
>
> For God, whom I serve [worship] in my spirit in the preaching of the gospel of His Son, is my witness. (Romans 1:9)

I am being poured out as a drink offering upon the sacrifice and service of your faith. (Philippians 2:17)

I am amply supplied, having received from Epaphroditus what you have sent, a fragrant aroma, an acceptable sacrifice, well-pleasing to God. (Philippians 4:18)

Through Him then, let us continually offer up a sacrifice of praise to God, that is, the fruit of lips that give thanks to His name. And do not neglect doing good and sharing, for with such sacrifices God is pleased. (Hebrews 13:15–16)

For I am already being poured out as a drink offering, and the time of my departure has come. (2 Timothy 4:6)

In each of these passages Paul uses the vernacular of Hebraic worship to describe spiritual acts. He sees worship as wholly integrated into all of living. He may not be inferring there were no gatherings where people worship. In fact, those gatherings *might* well have been assumed as a common experience among believers. Yet Paul continually draws spirituality out of the temple and into the temples (his people)—out of religious ecclesiasticism into the marketplace, the home, the field, and the prisons.

Paul even saw his death as an act of worship! We can easily see that when Christ taught that worship would become a 24/7, anywhere/ everywhere event that He didn't mean the diluted, self-indulging way we sometimes use the word *worship* ("Oh, I worship out here every Sunday morning on the golf course"). Rather, every day the believer who lives in this new kingdom of freedom reflects the glory of God. He is liberated to breathe fresh, free air, and everywhere he goes he can experience worship. This is a new existence altogether, a fresh essential life of living worship.

All of life is an act of worship when "sacrificed" to God. We cannot explore the concept at length here—that would demand an entire study in the book of Romans. But Christ's teaching was preparing us for the second chapter of Acts. It is *His* sacrifice that made the second chapter of Acts possible—opening the heavens for the kingdom of God to come here on earth. And the Holy Spirit fulfilled Christ's teaching with a demonstration of His "really real" power in the lives of humans just like you and me.

"Living worship" means a worship that is alive. It also means walking out our worship in the new kingdom of freedom. It sounds like a great idea, but is it too idealistic? What does this mean in practical terms? Let's keep it simple: Simple acts of living worship make absolutely no sense in the economy of this world, but they are the essential currency of the kingdom of heaven. These are the simple things that honor God, who is a real person accepting these sacrifices and smiling on His children who do them.

We live our worship when we visit and help the vulnerable, such as widows, orphans, and the imprisoned, in their distress: "Pure and undefiled religion in the sight of our God and Father is this" (James 1:27). Our calling is to continually offer our sacrifices in these temples, our bodies, with praise and thanksgiving. Ours is to "do good and share," for these are sacrifices as well. We worship when we dance; we worship when we obey our leaders and protect the unity of the Lord's body. We worship when we shout His glories and when we refuse to get tired of doing what is right. Our generosity in giving becomes a burnt offering with a pleasing aroma to God.

Living worship is restricted to only one particular location: the place where you are. Wherever your temple is you can worship—because the temple is *you*. The personal presence of God dwells there. Living worship is not restricted to special seasons or days of celebration. We live worship moment by moment in the presence of the Lord, honoring Him in our hearts. We live worship when we are open to allowing God to awe us in the everyday.

Religious acts of sacrifice are ugly—like the Pharisees making themselves up to make sure everyone realized they were fasting. But quiet, simple acts of living worship are a sweet aroma to the Lord's nostrils. Giving in such a way that the left hand doesn't know what the right hand is doing. Privately doing good for someone who is your enemy. Sharing the story of Christ with someone. Speaking words of thanks and praise into a room that looks empty to your eyes but which you believe in your spirit is filled with the Lord. Asking Someone you can't see for something you don't have. Laying hands on and praying for someone's healing even though you fear they may reject you. This is living worship.

Living worship embraces the depth of the riches that are ours in Christ—both of the wisdom and knowledge of God. It embraces His judgments. It is open to embracing His uncertain, unfathomable ways in our lives. His ways only appear uncertain to our fleshly eyes; they are, in fact, an absolute certainty, as certain as the rising of the sun. Though they are sometimes uncomfortable, usually they're downright undiluted pleasure! This is not dead liturgy or legalistic, loveless good works. This is genuine. This is absolute nonsense to the dying world, but you are encountering the really real. This is living worship.

But there is another layer to this business of living worship. We are told that this process of living worship is crafting us for a living destiny.

Living Stones

When Solomon built the temple there were specific instructions regarding the stonemasonry. Stones were to be quarried and fitted off-site. There was not to be the sound of hammer and chisel meeting stone on the site of the temple. This was the Lord's specific instruction (1 Kings 6:7).

Fast forward to 1 Peter 2:4-5, where Peter speaks of Christ being a "living stone," rejected by men but precious in God's sight:

> You also, as living stones, are being built up as a spiritual house for a holy priesthood, to offer up spiritual sacrifices acceptable to God through Jesus Christ.

And Paul, while imprisoned in Rome, writes to the Ephesian believers (Ephesians 2:19–22):

> You are no longer strangers and aliens, but you are fellow citizens with the saints, and are of God's household, having been built on the foundation of the apostles and prophets, Christ Jesus Himself being the corner stone, in whom the whole building, being fitted together, is growing into a holy temple in the Lord, in whom you also are being built together into a dwelling of God in the Spirit.

Did you really hear that? We are being built into a temple where God dwells in the Spirit! Our destiny isn't the hereafter—it's not "pie in the sky." This is something going on right now. He's got a plan in mind, a future that involves us. He's chipping off my rough places so I can fit smoothly next to you. He's placing us carefully on a foundation laid by the apostles and prophets. He's squaring us all up—all tribes and nations. He's squaring us up by how He positioned the cornerstone— our Elder Brother, Jesus Christ.

And we're not inanimate stones, we're living stones. He is actively involved in our lives throughout our years, day-to-day, moment-by-moment. When the kingdom of this earth was invaded by the kingdom of heaven He made His plan clear for all to see: Christ Jesus did not come merely to take us to heaven; He came to take over the world! One-by-one, He's impregnating a bunch of living stones with the very DNA of God's Spirit. This spiritual DNA assures us that we'll grow to fit together properly because we're confident we will grow up to look like our Father and Elder Brother. Philippians 1:6 says, "I am confident of this very thing, that He who began a good work in you will perfect it until the day of Christ Jesus."

Sometimes I compare this spiritual identity that assures us of God's work in us to our own DNA. For better or for worse my son will grow up to resemble me. He doesn't have to *try* to look like me, he just will. Why? Because he's been bearing my DNA since his conception. Sure, he can go out of his way to avoid looking like me (and sometimes he does). He can dye his hair and wear contacts to change the color of his eyes. But he can't help it—something more powerful than all of that is at work *in* him.

I have an opinion about why stones were not to be chiseled at the temple's site. I think it is related to how God views worship and intimacy. God is greatly interested in fashioning us into the right shape to be fitted to a living temple. But when we come to Him for worship and fellowship He wants it to be a time and place for relationship, not work. What parent among us chooses to correct and instruct their child when he or she comes to express love and gratitude? Do any of us teach or scold our little ones when they come to wrap their arms around our necks? Of course not! So why would we expect our Father in heaven, who is a far better parent than we are, to refine us during times of intimacy?

There is a medieval carving by an unknown master in the Museum Mayer van den Bergh in Antwerp, Belgium. I find it fascinating and inspiring. It is called "St. John Resting on Jesus' Chest." It is unpretentious and unadorned—simply depicting Christ and the apostle John sitting on a bench. John's head rests on Christ's chest; his eyes are closed in devotion and peace. His right hand rests in Christ's hand while Jesus' other arm rests lovingly atop John's shoulder. Art critics recognize the spirituality of this work. They immediately see that the two figures form a single entity. With no space between them, arms and hands merging, their robes seem to flow into one another—the perfect picture of intimacy, unity, and rest. How is it that John enjoyed such favor and access? I believe it's because he released himself from religious ritual and the awareness of his own weaknesses and sin and learned to enjoy Jesus for himself—not the idea of a Savior or a theological construct but rather the Person who extended to him, and us, unimaginable love. I'm convinced that Christ has a big chest. He can let millions of us rest there.

Living worship rests. Living worship resists any delusion that these simple acts of worship can save us. Works do not—a Person does. He was sufficient to save us. He is sufficient to sanctify us until we are glorified. If we abandon the simplicity of our faith in Him we become as foolish as the Galatians. They had a whole book in the Bible dedicated to correcting their foolishness—the idea that Christ saves you but works keep you.

At all costs, we must resist the idea that acts—privately or corporately—can save us. They can't *keep* us in the kingdom of God either, or garner a seat for us closer to Christ at the head of the table. Works don't work. Our best shot is rotting rags. And I can't buy anything in this kingdom with a currency of rags. My currency is *given* to me through the benevolence of my Father.

This is rest for all of you who are weary of trying to be a Christian. This is release for all of you who have carried the burden of shame even though somehow you know Christ has forgiven you. But this is bad news for the legalists; their religious charade no longer impresses. They can no longer wrap themselves in a cloak of good works and look down on the broken, the spiritually destitute, sinners, or Christians that make the mistake of being human. No matter whether you are burdened with shame or you are burdening others with it—please forgive as God has forgiven. Stop backsliding from grace back into works!

Martin Luther writes powerfully about passive righteousness in his *Introduction to Romans*.[1] He recognizes that what God brought to the table is abundant grace and all we've brought to the table is what He wanted most: *us*. This truth unties the knot in our chests to breathe free air, to rest in our new identity and live freely. I guarantee that if you "exhale" your preoccupations and religious notions and "inhale" God's acceptance and freedom you will naturally respond with living worship. The response to condemnation is guilt. The response to grace and mercy is to share grace and mercy with others.

Remember King David from our earlier discussion? I believe one of the things the Lord loved so much about him was that he was so bold as to embrace God's acceptance of him. This freed him to deal honestly with God as a real person. To make this clearer, let me tell you, as radio commentator Paul Harvey would always say, "the *rest* of the story." See if you would even associate with King David once you knew more about him. Let's imagine your pastor standing before this Sunday's congregation to make this announcement:

"Next week we have a special guest leading us in worship. He is a skillful musician who served successfully in the military, killing tens of thousands. Consequently, he became a national political leader. As a leader, he fought many successful conquests, then became sexually entangled with the wife of one of his most trusted military leaders. Attempting a cover-up, he had his mistress's husband murdered. Later, he confessed his sin. God was gracious to forgive him and reinstated him. I just wanted you to know what to expect next Sunday: Our guest worship leader likes to play instruments, sing, dance, shout, clap his hands, and bow down in silence when he leads worship. He'll cheer you toward doing all these things as well. He's really quite emotional and moody because of the pressures he's under, so the service may involve a lot of sadness and crying in worship. Other times he's deliriously happy, so don't be surprised if he gets a bit reckless and takes some of his clothes off."

But David knew who he was, and he was at peace with that. Moreover, he knew who God was and was assured by that. David was walking out his life with a Person, and he showed the full range of his heart in his expression and communication with God. There was no sanctimony or ecclesiastical ascent in his blood-and-guts, laughter-and-tears worship. He was *living* it.

I admire that in him. In fact, I'd like to live worship that freely. Here—you hold my robe!

Key Points:

**All of life is an act of worship when "sacrificed" to God.
Living worship rests.**

Scripture:

Therefore I urge you, brethren, by the mercies of God, to
present your bodies a living and holy sacrifice, acceptable to
God, which is your spiritual service of worship.

Romans 12:1

Questions:

Do I define my worship by my day-to-day living?

Am I open to how I might live worship today?

Do I rest in my identity in Christ? *Really?*

✦✦✦✦✦✦✦✦✦✦

ADDITIONAL RESOURCES:

Edwards, Gene. *100 Days in the Secret Place*. Shippensburg, Pa.: Destiny Image Publishers, 2002.

Johnson, Bill. *When Heaven Invades Earth*. Shippensburg, Pa.: Treasure House (Destiny Image Publishers), 2003.

Luther, Martin. *Introduction to Romans*. Available as a download at *www.johnrandalldennis.com*.

MacDonald, George. *Knowing the Heart of God*. Minneapolis, Minn.: Bethany House Publishers, 2000.

CHAPTER 11

Simple Acts of Worship

I CONSIDERED CALLING this chapter "Simple Acts of Foolishness" because acts of worship are absurd to the wisdom of this world. But as surely as the Bible admonishes us to live worship by good works that express our faith in everyday life, it also urges us to participate in physical expressions of worship that are consistent with our faith. The new covenant did not abolish the old covenant—it fulfilled it. So the first Christians did not stop worshiping in the temple as they had before. They continued to worship in the temple with the same expressions as before. But now they also worshiped in spirit and in truth in their newly indwelt temple—themselves.

In most biblical passages there appears to be a "physiology" of worship—physical expressions of spiritual things, or real expressions of really real things. Around the emphasis of a heart and life devoted to God, the Bible portrays expressions of worship and praise in posture (bowing, dancing, standing, etc.), expressions of the hands (raised, clapping, etc.), use of the voice (shouting, singing, or being silent), and more. Though our cultural frame of reference may make us uneasy with many of these biblical expressions, I believe they are a vital connection with the kingdom of freedom.

C. S. Lewis recognizes this in his book *The Screwtape Letters,* which contains humorous letters of advice from a senior experienced demon to his younger nephew, Wormwood. The human that Wormwood has been assigned to has become a Christian. One of the first things that Screwtape suggests to his nephew is how to keep the human from encountering the "really real" by keeping him preoccupied with the *ordinary*:

> Thanks to the processes which we set at work in them centuries ago, they find it all but impossible to believe in the unfamiliar while the familiar is right before their very eyes. Keep pressing home on him the *ordinariness* of things. Above all, do not attempt to use sciences—they will positively encourage him to think about realities he can't touch or see; don't let him get away from that invaluable "real life."[1]

Later Screwtape drives home an important point about tempting him away from simple acts of worship:

> They can be persuaded that bodily position makes no difference to their prayers; for they constantly forget, what you must always remember, that they are animals and whatever their bodies do affects their souls. It is funny how mortals always picture us as putting things into their minds: in reality our best work is done by keeping things out.[2]

Expressive worship affects our souls. I believe old Screwtape is dangerously insightful about human nature. He drives home a valid point. What we do with our bodies, our simple acts of worship (or lack of them), tells our souls something significant. I'll go one step further: Not only do we tell our souls something but our physical engagement also proclaims something before men and to the countless unseen. And further still: When we worship we become active partners in God's will being done on earth as it is in heaven. They do bow down to Him in heaven, don't they? They do lift holy hands in prayer and sing—right?

To be sure, the prophets tell us how much God deeply disdains acts of worship when our hearts are far from Him in blatant spiritual infidelity. Moreover, Christ warns that it's quite possible to go through these expressions as religious playacting before others, before God, or even before ourselves. But when we genuinely give honor to Him with our bodies, whether by dancing or by serving the poor, it is difficult to go through these acts without their profoundly impacting us to the core. We are not simply working ourselves into an emotional froth; we are being transforming by God's indwelling presence. We engage the kingdom of heaven by such expressions.

I can hear some traditionalists saying, "June, I knew it! Quick—hide the kids! He's one of *those*." These Christians have told me that expressive worship—incorporating acts of bowing, lifting our hands, or other such expressions—is not universal and spiritual but merely a historic/cultural (specifically, Old Testament Jewish) expression. They struggle with worship leaders who would have the audacity to encourage them to lift their hands, applaud the Lord, or (shudder!) shout. These people would have had a severe problem with King David and much of the corporate worship described in the Bible. I believe they'll have some adjustments to make in heaven. I know I will because I am not, by nature, a shouter.

On the other hand, I get the exact same response from the other end of the spectrum when I start telling contemporary worshipers about the value and power of creeds and liturgy in worship: "Whoa—dude! He's one of *those*! Let's get outta here!" Many believe that sincere worship cannot embrace any traditional worship forms such as ancient Christian practices, creeds, rites, or hymns. I believe there is no such thing as dead liturgy, only lethargic Christians. I believe in the power of uttered truths in whatever form they take.

EXPRESSIVE WORSHIP AFFECTS OUR SOULS.

I guess that makes me an Equal Opportunity Offender. Both groups disdain any activity they see as artificial. Both groups can skate right past the issue of truth. Both expression and tradition play important parts in corporate worship. Either group that excludes the other misses out on something vital.

To stoics who resist more physical expression, I offer the following questions to consider:

- If physical bowing and expression are not important, why are they vital to the worship we see throughout the Psalms, or to the angels and elders in Revelation?
- Why was the physical act of bowing down of such importance to Daniel, to Shadrach, Meshach, and Abednego that they were willing to die rather than bow before earthly kings? Remember that first-century Christians were not persecuted because they bowed to Christ but rather because they refused to bow to Caesar.

- "All these things I will give you if you bow down and worship me" (Matthew 4:9). If posture is simply a cultural matter, why was it such a big deal to Satan? Why on earth did he stipulate to Jesus that He not only acknowledge Satan but also bow down to him?

I believe physical expression has greater significance in the unseen spiritual realm than we realize. I believe such expressions are points at which the real and the really real intersect. The importance of this is underscored both by example and instruction. They are found throughout the entire Bible but examples are most common in the Psalms. Look at the following passages. They are by no means exhaustive, but see if you don't agree with noted worship author Dr. Robert Webber that worship is not mere intellectual assent to the idea of ascribing worth to God. "Worship is a verb."[3]

Proclaim! (Sometimes in Vigorous Song!)

Sing to the Lord, all the earth; proclaim good tidings of His salvation from day to day. (1 Chronicles 16:23)

We hear them in our own tongues speaking of the mighty acts of God. (Acts 2:11)

I have proclaimed glad tidings of righteousness in the great congregation; Behold, I will not restrain my lips, O LORD, You know. (Psalm 40:9)

It is good to give thanks to the Lord and to sing praises to Your name, O Most High; to declare Your lovingkindness in the morning and Your faithfulness by night, with the ten-stringed lute and with the harp, with resounding music upon the lyre. (Psalm 92:1–3 *A song for the Sabbath day*)

Shout to the Lord— Praise His Name!

And now my head will be lifted up above my enemies around me, and I will offer in His tent sacrifices with shouts of joy; I will sing, yes, I will sing praises to the LORD. (Psalm 27:6)

Sing to Him a new song; play skillfully with a shout for joy. (Psalm 33:3)

Shout joyfully to God, all the earth; sing the glory of His name; make His praise glorious. (Psalm 66:1)

O come, let us sing for joy to the LORD, let us shout joyfully to the rock of our salvation. (Psalm 95:1)

Bow Down!

But as for me, by Your abundant lovingkindness I will enter Your house, at Your holy temple I will bow in reverence. (Psalm 5:7)

Raise Your Hands!

I lift up my hands toward Your holy sanctuary. (Psalm 28:2)

So I will bless You as long as I live; I will lift up my hands in Your name. (Psalm 63:4)

Lift up your hands to the sanctuary and bless the LORD. (Psalm 134:2)

Clap!

O clap your hands, all peoples; shout to God with the voice of joy. (Psalm 47:1)

Sing!

Sing to Him, sing praises to Him; speak of all His wonders. (1 Chronicles 16:9)

But let all who take refuge in You be glad, let them ever sing for joy. (Psalm 5:11)

I will give thanks to the LORD according to His righteousness and will sing praise to the name of the LORD Most High. (Psalm 7:17)

I will be glad and exult in You; I will sing praise to Your name, O Most High. (Psalm 9:2)

Play Instruments!

Sing to Him a new song; play skillfully with a shout of joy. (Psalm 33:3)

The singers went on, the musicians after them, in the midst of the maidens beating tambourines. (Psalm 68:25)

Raise a song, strike the timbrel, the sweet sounding lyre with the harp. (Psalm 81:2)

Praise Him with trumpet sound; praise Him with harp and lyre. Praise Him with timbrel and dancing; praise Him with the stringed instruments and pipe. Praise Him with loud cymbals; praise Him with resounding cymbals. (Psalm 150:3–5)

Dance!

Let them praise His name with dancing; let them sing praises to Him with timbrel and lyre. (Psalm 149:3)

If this doesn't look and sound like your worship, you're missing out. You're missing out on the very same expressions that ring in the heavens. You're missing an opportunity to draw back the curtain of the real to encounter the really real Person right at the center of it all. Don't let the singing be kept to trained vocalists. And don't let dancing be limited to trained dancers. These all are expressions you can enjoy! C. S. Lewis said once that the reason we have solos is for the ridiculous reason that some people sing better than the rest of us. Don't let the soloists have all the fun just because they can sing better!

But let me press in further: Do we send ourselves mixed messages by reading Psalms and lyrics that say similar things, and then proceed to *not* do it? Why on earth do we sing "Come let us worship and bow down; let us kneel before the Lord our God, our Maker" (Psalm 95:6) as we stand there frozen? Why would we say or sing "Shout to the Lord"

(Darlene Zschech) and not shout? We often structure our worship services in such a way that we sing something while providing no opportunity for the congregation to *do* what they are singing. Or why sing "Be still, and know that I am God" (Psalm 46:10 NIV) or "My soul waits in silence for God" (Psalm 62:1) and then not stop to allow ourselves some time for silence and waiting?

When we sing or speak one thing and do another we send mixed messages to our souls. And when we send ourselves these mixed messages in worship, should it surprise us when we are likewise disconnected in our Christian walk? Is it any surprise when we don't live worship by sharing the joy of the Good News, healing the sick, or visiting the imprisoned and infirmed? We make of ourselves spiritual frauds by being hearers of the Word and not doers. In our healthy interest in "being" instead of doing, we can become spiritual couch potatoes (I call them "pew potatoes"). We confess a word we do not do.

Of course I am not prescribing outward acts of worship or disingenuous liturgy to disguise wayward hearts. But this is a fact of my personal experience: I can command my body to be in sync with the truth I embrace in spirit and in truth—and then my soul will follow by getting in sync with my body. I sometimes feel like avoiding exercise at all costs, but once I begin a good walk my attitude changes—have you had that happen? Ever tell yourself to sit up straight and change your posture and suddenly you realize you're thinking clearer? Our bodies really do telegraph messages to our minds and emotions.

There is still one area we should cover before we leave this discussion: safety. You are safe in the presence of God to express yourself. You are safe to explore expression and make some mistakes. You are safe to express your frustration with your situation in life and even with God.

Worshipers can safely express themselves entirely. When we express ourselves in worship, we are free to express everything honestly. We often have severe difficulty in expressing emotions in worship that we don't want to face or we don't think are acceptable. That is simply wrong-headed religious thinking. Among the expressions we especially avoid are frustration or questioning God. It seems that in our contemporary religious culture we lend wings to all kinds of expression that we have deemed godly and deny ourselves those that are human. Many times it's part of building up our religious world of denial.

Such was not the case in biblical worship. Time and time again the book of Psalms jars us with the frankness of King David's frustration with God. The Old Testament is replete with many examples of people complaining to God—Job, Ezekiel, Isaiah, Jeremiah, and the list goes on. They all seemed to think that God was big enough to take raw honesty, whether it was ecstatic in nature or seething. We approve of joy and praise. We write regal hymns of laud or choruses of energetic praise. But we find it convenient and comfortable to avoid subjects such as anger, loneliness, and despair altogether.

This ought to be a focal point of our prayers: *Lord, help us to worship you in truth, fully recognizing that truth is sometimes uncomfortable. Help us to be honest worshipers. Help us to avoid "feel-good Christianity" at all costs and to embrace worshiping in spirit and in truth right where we are.* Believe me, He's secure enough to listen to any honest thing you want to tell Him.

Key Points:

Expressive worship affects our souls.
Worshipers can safely express themselves entirely.

Scripture:

How long, O Lord? Will You forget me forever?
Psalm 13:1

Questions:

What things have I been telling my soul in my acts of worship?
Is there any honest issue I have avoided expressing to God?

✦✦✦✦✦✦✦✦✦✦

ADDITIONAL RESOURCES:

Lewis, C. S. *The Screwtape Letters*. London: Collins Fontana Books, 1964.

Webber, Robert E. *Worship Is a Verb*. Peabody, Mass.: Hendrickson Publishers, Inc., 1992.

CHAPTER 12

A Fresh Commission

WE'VE COME A LONG WAY since we started looking at worship together. I hope you've come to see that worship isn't music, and it isn't merely a twenty-minute segment in a church service before a sermon. It's not a form and it's not works. It is a multidimensional response to God that focuses on His persons and His works. It really is a diamond of many facets. And I hope you've come to see that the "worship wars" in many of our churches miss the point altogether. The Enemy uses these squabbles to distract us from the really real.

You need to know something about books, tapes, and seminars. It's a statistical fact that of all the people reading and listening to people like me, only around 3 percent (sometimes it's as high as 10 percent) actually *do* the things authors and speakers encourage them to do. But that's only a "real" statistic. The Holy Spirit is "really real." I assure you that if Christ wasn't restrained by the real laws of physics (you step into water, not *on* it), the Spirit won't give a moment's thought to the real statistics of reader retention.

When Peter addressed the multitude on Pentecost the Holy Spirit showed up. Peter didn't bag between 3 percent and 10 percent for the kingdom that day. God doesn't release 3 percent of the captives who cry out to Him, and Christ didn't feed only 10 percent of the crowd on the mountainside. You're not going to be left in a nameless, faceless 97 percent—you're about to defy the laws of nature!

Why? Because **God is looking for you.** Surprised? You may not realize that, and you may not *feel* that way right now—but He really is.

Here is an absolutely mind-blowing teaching of Christ:

> True worshipers will worship the Father in spirit and truth;
> *for such people the Father seeks to be his worshipers.* (John 4:23,
> emphasis mine)

You don't have to labor and struggle to find Him. He doesn't need you to fast, pour ashes on your head, take a vow of silence, or hold a prayer vigil. *You* may need those things to convince your heart through physical expression of your intense need of God, but God doesn't need them to get through to you.

God is drawn irresistibly to true worshipers. The truth is, He can't stay away from them. It's like when I go to the store to pick up milk but find myself searching for a Heath bar. I don't need a Heath bar. I need milk. But my love for the delicious treat sends me looking for it anyway. Of course, God doesn't *need* you or anything else in the way we think of need. He is sufficient in and of himself. But when He thinks about us He can't help but pursue us. Sure, I know this is a flimsy illustration, using my love for a particular candy bar. But it doesn't fail as an illustration because it's frivolous (though it certainly is); it fails because it does not begin to portray *how much* God loves you. You are much more than an indulgence, a fancy, to Him!

He can't help expressing His lovingkindness toward us. You'd think our behavior would have discouraged Him by now. But it just oozes out of Him because He doesn't just love, He *is* love. He just keeps on loving you and being attracted by your sincere worship. He's not actually seeking your worship—He's seeking *you*.

And you watch. If you worship Him without pretense, if you genuinely humble yourself and prostrate your life before Him, He'll be sure to respond by making himself known to you. If you break up the fallow ground of sin and arrogance, cultivating a heart of authentic humility, the Lord will rain righteousness down on you. I just know it! How? Because Christ plainly told us, "Hey, you want to know who the Father chases? Those who worship Him in spirit and in truth" (John 4:23, paraphrased).

We started this study of worship with the Lord's promise in Jeremiah that if we search with all our hearts He will be found of us (Jeremiah 29:13–14). But wait a minute—there's a twist here. We're searching for Him, but I don't believe He's hiding at all. The only thing hiding Him is *us. We're* hiding Him. So, ironically, that's why we must search for Him. He's so big and so willing to be found that even our own attempts to hide Him from ourselves will ultimately fail.

Here's the truth: "The eyes of the Lord move to and fro throughout the earth that He may strongly support those whose heart is completely His" (2 Chronicles 16:9). If your heart is His, He's got your number. It's only a matter of time until you've got His.

This is great news, isn't it? So I want to offer you a fresh commission: **Just worship!** It doesn't matter if you use hymns or choruses—just worship Him. He doesn't care if you bring your Book of Common Prayer along or use a more informal approach. He just wants to visit with you. Praise Him with your pipe organs or with your praise bands, worship with your hymnals or worship with your overhead projections—but above all, worship with your spirit.

Worship Sunday morning and in prayer meetings, worship in Mass, worship at your crusades and revivals, with your CD players, or in your cathedrals . . . but worship! Don't approach God as though you were a consumer, focusing on musical preferences and things that please you. You can't allow yourself the luxury of waiting for Sunday morning or worship sculpted to your preferences—not if you're hungry for God. Worship Him right now as a humble child, seeking only Him, your benevolent Father, and His good pleasure.

And when you worship don't act like you're the only one there. Behave like He's present and remember that He's not a mist but a Person . . . because He really is. Focus on vital things that matter and commit to engaging yourself in simple acts of worship. Then expect Him to show up. Engage in spiritual disciplines if it helps awaken your slumbering spirit from the *ordinary* to become spiritually sensitive. Give up the "stuff" that gets in the way of authentic worship.

If you'll get involved in these things I know you'll train your heart to encounter a "really real" Person. You'll receive a deeper and clearer revelation of Him. If you're thirsty, come—come on! If you're hungry, come. Even if you have no money, come on anyway—come and buy with nothing. Just as paradoxically, He'll always satisfy you, and yet you'll always want more.

Live your worship by singing for Him. Clap for Him, dance for Him. Proclaim living words of His glory. Stretch yourself beyond what you thought worship was to what worship is. Raise your hands to Him, pray to Him, eat His flesh and drink His blood together. Speak living words in Scriptures, rites, and creeds. Lift banners to Him, light candles for Him, yell for Him, be silent for Him. But worship.

Live worship behind closed doors when it's only you and Him. Live it in your church community. Live your worship in your schools, at the office, at the grocery store, at Starbucks. Don't be afraid to make mistakes—God isn't keeping a worship scorecard. Don't be afraid to be honest with Him about anything at all—He loves our transparency. When you drop the pretense you'll come to realize that He's not ashamed of you. He doesn't simply love you in a generic sort of way—He actually likes you, warts and all. He's the one who would say, "Why don't we go get a cup of coffee and hang out for a while?" And when you start living worship based on that rock-bottom assurance, you'll see God's kingdom increase in you, in your family, in your church, and in your neighborhood. Live worship moment by moment, wherever you go.

If you've allowed yourself to be distracted or tied down by rules and expectations, you've missed out on so much. But you can start right now. This is a fresh moment. Whoever you are, wherever you are, no matter what time it is, simply bow down in your heart before Him. Tell Him the truths about Him you really believe to the core, whether your emotions tell you they're true or not. Tell Him honestly what you can believe right now and ask Him to help in the places where you have unbelief. (Like the boy's father did in Mark 9:24.)

This is a moment for spiritual honesty, not religious role playing. Tell Him you want to know Him as He really is—not the made-up person you thought He was. Tell Him you're not going to try to be "acceptable" anymore but you are willing to be accepted. And invite Him: *Holy Spirit, come. Come with all your faithfulness, come with all your love, come with your gifts. I've decided that what I really want is you and whatever you intend for me. Come. I won't resist you. You don't have to come the way I thought you would either. Just come.* Don't wait for a church service or a churchy place. Find some private place and let your worship begin to flow. Begin by reading this Scripture, and listen for a while afterward:

The Holy Spirit says, "TODAY IF YOU HEAR HIS VOICE, DO NOT HARDEN YOUR HEARTS" (Hebrews 3:7–8).

Don't let unbelief hold you back. This is your moment. Just worship.

✦✦✦✦✦✦✦✦✦✦

ADDITIONAL RESOURCES:

Phillips, J. B. *Your God Is Too Small*. New York: MacMillan Publishing Co., Inc., 1961.

Redman, Matt. *The Unquenchable Worshiper*. Ventura, Calif.: Regal Books, 2001.

Webber, Robert E. *Journey to Jesus*. Nashville: Abingdon Press, 2002.

Endnotes

CHAPTER 1
1. Madeleine L'Engle, *A Wrinkle in Time* (New York: Dell Publishing Co., 1962).
2. James Strong, *Strong's Concordance* (Nashville: Nelson Reference & Electronic Publishing, 1990).
3. Joan Comay and Ronald Brownrigg, *Who's Who in the Bible* (New York: Bonanza Books, 1980), 28, 336, 181, 345.

CHAPTER 2
1. Job 1:21.

CHAPTER 3
1. Isaiah 6:7.
2. C. S. Lewis, *The Lion, the Witch, and the Wardrobe* (New York: HarperCollins, 1994), 64.

CHAPTER 4
1. 2 Samuel 6:1–23, paraphrased.
2. John Piper, *Desiring God* (Sisters, Ore.: Multnomah, 2003).

CHAPTER 5
1. 2 Chronicles 20:6–12, emphasis added.
2. 2 Chronicles 20:15–17.
3. 2 Chronicles 20:21, emphasis added.

CHAPTER 6
1. 1 Samuel 1:1–20, paraphrased.

CHAPTER 8
1. Acts 1:7–8.
2. Acts 1:11

CHAPTER 9

1. Revelation 1:10–11.

CHAPTER 10

1. Download at no cost at my Web site: *www.johnrandalldennis.com*.

CHAPTER 11

1. C. S. Lewis, *The Screwtape Letters* (London: Collins Fontana Books, 1964), 14.
2. Ibid., 25.
3. Robert E. Webber, *Worship Is a Verb* (Peabody, Mass.: Hendrickson Publishers, 1992).

Bring LIVING WORSHIP to your church.

Living Worship
EVENTS

Seminars &
Intimate Worship

with

JOHN RANDALL DENNIS

For complete information, visit:
www.johnrandalldennis.com

More Ways to Make
W O R S H I P
Vital to Your Life

Prepare to Be Transformed Through God's Love!

In *The Kiss of Heaven,* you'll discover how you can experience God's favor as you seek His blessing to pursue the dream He has planted in your heart. Darlene says, "God is watching for someone to kiss with His favor at this very moment. He watches—hoping to see our hands lifted up to love Him, and receive His help so He can demonstrate His loving power through us to a love-starved planet."

Kiss of Heaven by Darlene Zschech

Holy, Holy, Holy Is the Lord God Almighty. . . .

Enter into God's presence and Spirit with new passion when you discover what it means to play the part of Extravagant Worshiper. Darlene Zschech's fervent love for her Lord leaps from the page as she inspires you to take your church deeper into worship!

Extravagant Worship by Darlene Zschech